DOUBLE IDENTITY

DOUBLE IDENTITY

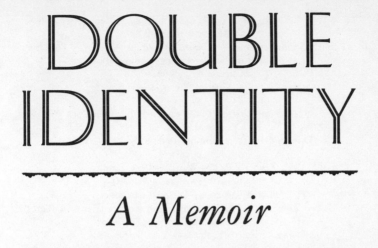

A Memoir

ZOFIA S. KUBAR

ɯ HILL AND WANG · NEW YORK

A division of Farrar, Straus and Giroux

Library of Congress Cataloging-in-Publication Data
Kubar, Zofia S.
Double identity: a memoir / Zofia S. Kubar.—1st ed.
p. cm.
1. Jews—Poland—Warsaw—Persecutions.
2. Holocaust, Jewish (1939–1945)—
Poland—Warsaw—Personal narratives.
3. Kubar, Zofia S.   4. Warsaw (Poland)—Ethnic relations.   I. Title.
DS135.P62W279   1989
940.53'15'0392404384—dc19   89—1991

Portions of this book have previously appeared, in different form,
in *The Jewish Spectator* and *Partisan Review*

Some of the names of persons described in this book have
been changed to protect their privacy

To the memory of my parents

Contents

DOUBLE IDENTITY

A Ghost of a Chance

I SPENT TWO AND A HALF YEARS of my life in the Warsaw ghetto. I survived the deportation in 1942. On January 18, 1943, in the second roundup,* I was ordered downstairs along with my friends and neighbors, pushed into a long column of people already standing in the street, and marched in the direction of the Umschlagplatz, the railroad siding where the cattle cars were waiting. We were each allowed to take a small package of food and a few possessions.

In the same row with me were my friends Marcel Reich

---

* The first "resettlement action"—a euphemism for transporting Jews to the gas chambers—took place from July 22 to September 21, 1942; about three hundred thousand Jews were deported from Warsaw to the Treblinka death camp. In the second action, from January 18 to January 23, 1943, about six thousand Jews were deported.

and his wife, Tosia; Rachel Singer, my young roommate; and Gustava Jarecka with her two small sons, Karol and Marek. One of the most brilliant young novelists in Poland before the war, Gustava had been working as a switchboard operator for the Judenrat,* a position she owed to its chairman, Adam Czerniakow, who tried to save some intellectuals by giving them jobs. During the first "action," verification of employment had sometimes helped people to escape deportation. But now, in the second "action," no job, however essential for war production, spared anyone.

Our column proceeded in silence. We believed we were headed for death, although we did not know when we would find it, or how. Then Marcel took over.

"We should run if we get the chance," he said.

Gustava refused, despairing, sure she couldn't make it with the children. She stayed in line when the rest of us made our move. We were passing a bombed-out building with crumbling steps leading down to a cellar. Marcel gave the signal. The Germans shot at us but missed. They didn't bother to chase us or waste more bullets on four Jews who would not escape their fate anyway. We reached the cellar and were safe for the time being. Later, we learned from the janitor of our building, who had managed to escape from the train, that Gustava had died en route, of suffocation under a pile of bodies.

After the January deportation, only about 65,000 Jews, out of about 450,000, were left in the ghetto. Frantically they weighed their chances: to stay there and share the

* Jewish Council, the body appointed by the German occupation authorities which was responsible for enforcing Nazi orders affecting the Jews and for administering the affairs of the Jewish community.

common fate, or to escape to the Aryan part of the city. Most, overcome by the apathy that fear produces, decided to stay. Many did not have Polish friends who could help, or the money to pay for a hideout. Then there were those who hesitated because they were still making money in the ghetto or were reluctant to sacrifice their belongings. The underground press had confirmed reports of the gas ovens, but most people refused to believe them; those who decided to remain in the ghetto wanted to deceive themselves and listened eagerly for "good news," the false rumors spread by the Germans and their agents. "Not everybody dies in the camps," they argued. "Those healthy enough to work will survive."

Stories circulated about those who had fled to the Aryan side and, once outside the wall, were surrounded by Polish blackmailers who took everything they possessed and then handed them over to the Gestapo. The fugitives were shot on the spot. This was true, but little was said about those who were lucky enough to escape.

My own chances of survival on the Polish side were slight. I had no money to pay for a hiding place or for ransom to the blackmailers. I was virtually a stranger in the city and I had only two Polish friends there. One, Mrs. Uklejska, had been the headmistress of the Gymnasium I had attended for a year before I went off to the university in Cracow. We had been out of touch for seven years, but when she learned by chance that I was in the ghetto she had visited me there, bringing food and offering help. The other was Szczęsny Dobrowolski, husband of my childhood friend Stefa. Stefa was Jewish and worked in the underground, her identity concealed by her marriage to a Pole. I could rely on these people, but a whole network of Polish friends was needed for even one Jew to survive outside the walls, and I knew no one else in Warsaw. True, some of my Gymnasium classmates might still be in the city, but I hadn't seen them in seven years. After I'd earned my degrees in Cracow—in law at the Jagiellonian University, in business at the Academy of Commerce—I had gone home to Lodz. Soon afterward, the war broke out and the city was occupied by the Nazis. The Russian border was temporarily open, and like thousands of other young people, I decided to escape to Soviet Russia. My parents encouraged me: it was commonly believed that the young, because they were likely to have been politically active, were most at risk.

I packed a rucksack with a few belongings, refused the money my parents tried to press on me, and headed east, stopping off briefly—or so I thought—in Warsaw. But I learned how much better off Jews were there—and elsewhere under the Generalgouvernement, in the territory occupied by the Germans—than they were in Lodz, which had been incorporated into the Reich. I therefore postponed my flight to Russia to arrange for my parents' move to Warsaw, but as they were preparing to leave, the Germans sealed off the Lodz ghetto. At the same time they closed the new German–Russian border. My parents were stuck in Lodz. I was stuck in Warsaw.

Now, three years later, I knew that time was running out. Doomed to annihilation, I was haunted by a dream that I was trying to leave but it was too late. The troops were again surrounding the ghetto to deport those who were left. Constantly I consulted my mirror for reassurance that I could pass for a Pole. It told me that I was 5′1″, slender, with brown eyes and dark blond hair. Flaxen hair and blue eyes would have been better. What bothered me most was my nose, not especially long, but not the small, upturned Polish kind. Would the shape of my nose determine my future? Because I was young, I told myself, I might survive in a camp. But because I was young I decided not to surrender to a fate assigned by the Nazis, whatever it might be. Once I had made my choice, I gave my Polish friends the signal that I was ready to move.

By now, virtually the only way to leave the ghetto was as a member of a labor brigade assigned to work outside. One day in early February I joined some fifty men and women at the Żelazna Gate, the official exit, at dawn. I wore as many layers of clothing as I could, ostensibly against the cold. The gendarmes who searched us paid no attention to this padding, and did not find the only valuables I owned—my Aunt Ida's ring with a small diamond, and a gold bracelet, a graduation gift from my parents. I had a little money given me by my uncle and my friends, just enough to tide me over until I found a job. I also smuggled out some family pictures and my two university diplomas. I knew it was ridiculous to want to keep this evidence of my education, since I would be another person on the Aryan side, but I was young enough to believe in a future after the war ended.

With the other women, I was assigned to wash windows in some apartments on Narbutta Street that were being made ready for German military families. At noon, during the break permitted by the guards, I met Mrs. Uklejska, who was waiting in a nearby grocery store, and gave her for safekeeping all the things I had smuggled out. Before I hurried back to work I managed to telephone Stefa's husband, who told me where to pick up my new birth certificate and gave me the address where I would be expected next time, when I left the ghetto for good.

Two days later I joined the brigade again, swaddled in more clothes. We washed windows until dusk, then lined up, some of us carrying potatoes or other food we were allowed to buy, for the trip back to the ghetto. I carried nothing. We marched in the middle of the street, attracting occasional glances from Polish passersby. As we were leaving Polna Street, I looked around: nobody was watching. Cautiously I stepped to the end of our column, removing from my sleeve the unsewn Star of David armband and slipping it into my pocket. In no time I was on the sidewalk, part of the Polish crowd. Then I walked, not too slowly, not too fast, to the nearest streetcar stop. As I boarded the first car that came along, I realized that I didn't know the fare. I dared not ask: every Warsavian knew what it was. I asked the conductor for a ten-trip booklet so that I could hand him a ten-zloty bill, expecting that it would more than cover it. I was right; he gave me the tickets and the change. Now I was a Polish passenger on a Polish streetcar. I was no longer Zofia Rubinstein. The story of Zofia Sielczak had begun.

With a Flower in My Hair

MY FIRST SHELTER in the city was one room and a kitchen, shared with my landlady, a Miss Okonska, with whom my friend Stefa had made the necessary arrangements. It was modestly furnished but spotlessly, almost painfully, clean. Miss Okonska had been a dressmaker, and she was impeccably groomed—not a wrinkle in her gray skirt and white blouse. In appearance, and in the rigidity of her daily routine, she resembled a nun. To tell the truth, this exaggerated devotion to tidiness made me uncomfortable. I soon stopped eating at home, lest a bread crumb fall on the shining floor. But I couldn't give up bathing. There was no bathroom, and one had to wash at the kitchen sink, without spilling a drop of water. Miss Okonska managed this easily, and I did my best. Sometimes when, in spite of my efforts, I splashed some water, I would hear her say in her thin, penetrating voice, "You people are so careless!"

First I swallowed this criticism of my clumsiness, but when she repeated "you people" I asked her whom she meant. She was a little embarrassed; she hadn't expected the question, probably didn't realize what was on her mind. After a pause, she explained that she meant rich people, who were used to servants. I sensed that, like many Poles, she identified Jews with the rich. Certainly she was not consciously critical of Jews; after all, she was giving me shelter, putting her own life in jeopardy, without receiving anything in return. Nevertheless, this slip revealed the prejudices deeply rooted in the minds of even the most generous people, people who helped Jews while still unable to accept them as belonging to the same species as themselves.

Miss Okonska was usually quiet but friendly, and the first weeks of my stay passed harmoniously enough. I spent most of my days outside, walking around, practicing my new Polish identity. In those days there were people who would scrutinize the faces of their fellows, studying their expressions, the way they carried themselves. Some looked for a victim to blackmail; others were driven by pure curiosity to see if they could spot a Jew. It was important to blend into the crowd.

I stopped wearing the glasses I had worn for years; they might attract attention to my face. Also, they made me look intellectual. True, there were Polish intellectuals, but they didn't have to worry that their appearance would give them away. For me it was doubly precarious. Intellectuals constituted a minority and I had to avoid being linked with any minority. I knew that intellectuals were special targets of the Nazis, as they have been for other totalitarian regimes before and since.

"You've got spectacles on your nose and autumn in your soul." I remembered this description of the narrator in one of Isaac Babel's stories. I knew that the autumn in my soul must be concealed. Although during the occupation the Poles were sad and depressed, the Jews' despair was far worse. I had to try to show none of my feelings.

For a while I tried to look inconspicuous: I wore a gray hat pulled low over my forehead and a dark coat. But this costume soon began to depress me and I went to the other extreme—vivid colors, heavy makeup, even a beauty spot on my face. I thought that if I seemed eager to attract men I would look more Aryan, because it would be assumed that Jewish girls had too much to worry about and would not care to flirt with strangers. But this pose didn't last long; I came to see that it was ridiculous. I stopped trying to bleach my hair, afraid someone might guess I was motivated not by feminine vanity but by the need to disguise darker, "Jewish" hair. Finally I abandoned all these artifices and concentrated on my expression. I forced myself to look carefree. "It's a beautiful day," I would tell myself. "Life is exciting."

I believe I mastered a look of cheerful confidence. The effect was more than external: I had summoned up this optimism to control my facial muscles and they in turn influenced my feelings. Since danger was constant, I had to keep renewing my inner powers of resistance. Later, when spring came, I would wear a flower in my hair like other Polish girls to express the hope for victory and peace.

But now it was February 1943 and I needed to find friends. There were some Jews living on the Aryan side who considered it an advantage to remain alone; it minimized the danger of being recognized and denounced. But usually these Jews had money and could pay for their hiding places. Many of my Polish friends had been socialists and were now in Russia. My friend Stefa was deeply involved in the underground and asked me not to contact her. There was my old headmistress, Mrs. Uklejska, who had already done so much. She and her family were also active in the resistance, helping other Jewish friends and former students and teachers. I knew I could count on her. However, she couldn't take me into her apartment. I had to find more Poles who were ready to give me a hand. This was extremely dangerous for them; if they were caught sheltering a Jew, or helping one in any way, they could be put to death. Even those who did nothing, but only withheld knowledge of a Jew's hiding place, risked deportation to a concentration camp.

I was embarrassed, looking up my old schoolmates after seven years; I had been too preoccupied with a boyfriend then to get to know the girls. I would never have approached them if I hadn't needed help. They turned out to be sympathetic but frightened, like most Poles. They were astonished that I was alive, and I began to feel that it had been somehow "unfair" of me to have survived, since now I posed a problem. I listened to stories, true and untrue, about their own predicaments. I was passed along from one acquaintance to another, and told I should understand why they could do nothing. And I understood.

But there were a few girls I had liked, who had liked me, and finally I found one who really welcomed me. Cesia Szczypińska lived with her prospective mother-in-law and worked in her electrical appliance store. Cesia's fiancé, a

Polish army officer, had escaped to England. His mother was not enthusiastic about my visits, but Cesia was strong-willed and we saw each other often. The store was in the poor outskirts of the city near Kercelak, an old flea market where now the black market flourished. One could get anything there: food, clothes, jewelry, dollars. The dealers used the telephone in the store, with Cesia's permission. She and I were polite to them and they were impressed by two such well-educated girls. They knew neither of us had any money, and they tried to help us by giving us goods to sell on commission. Cesia sometimes managed to make a sale, but I never did. What a disaster, she said, to be a Jew with a goyish head at such a time—that is, to be like a Pole, with no business sense. I agreed, but that's the way it was.

Weeks had passed since I had boarded that first streetcar, and I was getting to know the city. Then one evening two new lodgers, sisters, showed up at Miss Okonska's. They were Stefa's cousins, also from the ghetto. Miss Okonska had generously agreed to squeeze them in. Now there were four of us in the two rooms of the apartment, but I was glad to have the company of girls my own age, pleased that two more had escaped the ghetto. These two looked Jewish and would have to stay indoors all day. I did not suspect at first that their presence in the apartment would threaten my place, my first shelter. They came from an affluent Warsaw family and had managed to hold on to some of their possessions. Like me, they were eager to please our landlady, but unlike me, they could express their gratitude by giving her small presents—a scarf, a pocketbook—almost every day. It would be unfair to Miss Okonska to say that these gifts were the main reason she finally chose the girls over me, but it would be naïve to think their largesse played no role in her decision.

The girls wanted me to move out because they thought I was a potential danger to them. Since I was in and out, they said, I might attract the attention of a policeman or a blackmailer in the street. If one followed me, he would discover them. They persuaded Miss Okonska that I, who looked less Jewish, should be the one to leave. Ghetto refugees had a saying: "Better stay alone on the streetcar." The fewer Jews there were in a place, the safer each individual was.

I was learning that a common fate did not always create a feeling of solidarity, that sometimes it actually aroused hostility among competitors for survival. I had no hope of convincing Miss Okonska that her decision was unfair, that I was almost penniless and a stranger in the city, and not at all in a better position than the sisters. But I knew Miss Okonska was basically kind and wouldn't throw me out without finding me another place.

And she did find one. In the same building there was a small room intended for a concierge but occupied by an old lady who was a kind of ward of the Church. Miss Okonska introduced me to Miss Aniela Bijas, vouching for my character and withholding, of course, the crucial information that I was Jewish. This would be my second move on the Aryan side, and as the Hebrew saying goes, *"Meshane makom, meshane mazal"*—Change your place, change your luck.

At Aunt Aniela's

I T IS PLEASANT to recall that my new landlady liked me very much. After a few days she asked me to call her Aunt Aniela. God forbid I should call her Grandma! She had never married, and was very proud of her membership in a sisterhood of virgins called Maidens in White. She had worked since girlhood in the homes of rich families, who had encouraged her in this celibate state; indeed, required it. Maidservants deprived of male society were more dependable, more faithful; and with thousands of young girls in the overpopulated countryside looking for work, Aunt Aniela had accepted this condition, reluctantly at first, perhaps—later, wholeheartedly.

She was short and plump, in her late seventies or early eighties. She was poor as could be and completely alone, but she did not seem unhappy. I never noticed a trace of envy or jealousy. She deeply believed that "blessed are the poor . . . for theirs is the kingdom of heaven." Though she accepted every word preached by the Church and seemed completely fulfilled, my intrusion into her quiet life apparently awakened dormant maternal feelings and a longing for love. She accepted everything I told her about myself. I dared not tell her I was Jewish, since I had no idea how she would react to such a startling piece of information. I was Polish and Catholic.

My story and my new personality had been carefully worked out. I came from the countryside, where I had been a teacher. I could not pretend that I was uneducated: my language, behavior, and manners would have betrayed me. On the other hand, I could not admit to having studied at the university. That level of education would have made her suspicious of my need to share her room. However, it was quite plausible that I had studied in a teachers' seminary. Girls from peasant families with higher aspirations than domestic service could study in these institutions, where the fees were very low. After two years they received a license to teach in primary schools. Thus, I became a seminary graduate looking for a job in Warsaw. My "profession" allowed me to be educated neither too little nor too much for my present circumstances.

During my wanderings on the Aryan side I acquired a wide knowledge of the linguistic peculiarities of many different types of people. Every Jewish survivor became, like me, an expert in this kind of deception. We had to speak excellent Polish, but we needed as well a perfect knowledge of certain mistakes and colloquialisms peculiar to different milieux. And I had never realized how many nuances there were in manners, gestures, facial expressions, and jokes. We had to invent credible identities and sustain them in every particular. One mistake could be fatal.

It was important for me to have relatives. Only Jews did not speak of them; their family members were dead or in hiding. So I invented an old aunt in Zielonka, an outlying village. I was a very good niece and took great care of my aunt, "visiting" her often. Aunt Aniela, of course, approved of my solicitousness, but I had another purpose in mind. Since I was needed in Zielonka, I had an excellent excuse for not going to Sunday Mass with her. I might have betrayed myself there. Or, if I hadn't, I would have felt that I was somehow taking unfair advantage of the true believers, although I was utterly indifferent to all religions at the time. But this way I could go every Sunday to see my dear aunt in Zielonka. Aunt Aniela missed me very much, but assured me that I had her full blessing.

When I returned to the room we shared, Aunt Aniela usually offered me a portion of the thin soup provided by one of the Church charities. Made with a few carrots and potatoes, this soup and about half a pound of bread made up her daily diet. I appreciated her generosity, but I always refused the soup, saying I'd already eaten, even though I was often hungry. Unfortunately, she also treated me to spiritual food that I could not refuse—morality tales that she read aloud each day from her religious reader.

She particularly loved the story of the girl invited to a restaurant by two wicked men. There they had slipped sleeping pills into her beer, and once she was unconscious, they had raped her. Somehow the author of the story made the situation clear without offending innocent readers. This story was a thriller for Aunt Aniela; she feared this fate could befall me. I assured her that I did not meet men, did not frequent restaurants, and hated beer. I could admit this with a clear conscience, since I did not then have male acquaintances, I did not go to restaurants, and I had never cared for beer.

In our 9 × 12 room were two beds with straw mattresses. My few belongings hung on one wall. (I had left my better clothes with Mrs. Uklejska since they were too good for a poor girl from the countryside.) Aniela's Sunday black skirt and crimson blouse hung on the opposite wall. Under her bed was a cardboard box in which she kept her festive dress—the outfit she would wear in her coffin. She showed it to me more than once, with innocent pride. Between the beds stood a small iron stove called for some unknown reason a "she-goat." It would have warmed us if we had had enough coal, but the amount we received from Catholic charities was barely enough to heat the soup on its only burner. We both suffered from the cold. Nevertheless, I could not give up the strange habit of my former life—washing myself daily. Miss Aniela could not understand; she was shocked at the sight of my naked body. Why must I scrub all over? Such a practice suggested women of easy virtue. And I was such a decent, honest girl. Finally, love overcame prejudice, and she began to fetch me a pot of warm water each evening from a neighbor. I used a small basin. She did not mind my splashing water on the floor.

After the bath, it was time for evening prayers. Every good Catholic prayed before bedtime. When Aunt Aniela knelt to pray, I would jump into bed. She did not like this at all.

"Dear child," she would say, "every creature praises God. The cow moos, *moo-moo*, and praises God. The bird twitters, *tschwirr-tschwirr*, and praises God. And you, my bad girl, you do not want to do it?"

I would explain that it was cold and I would pray in bed. She did not approve, but she indulged my whim.

I was getting used to my new personality. Now when I think about life at Aunt Aniela's I can't remember whether I thought of it as a hardship. I always had the ability to adjust to new circumstances. I am sure that I blotted out the memory of my room in my parents' house in Lodz. Now I remember it from time to time, seeing it full of light. There was the flowered wallpaper, the white furniture fashionable in my childhood, and a desk that could be adjusted to my height. There were many books on the shelves—most of them I remember to this day—and a cabinet where I kept my toys. I remember the pictures on the walls: a big photograph of myself, a five-year-old with curly hair and a look of surprise on her face and a wooden wheel, then a very popular toy, in her hands. There were prints of smiling children in a garden, at the lake, on a beach. The decor showed no great artistic taste on the part of my parents, but everything was arranged with loving care. I never thought of the room in the days when I moved from shelter to shelter.

Although I liked my good Aunt Aniela, there were moments when playing the role of a naïve, cheerful girl was unbearable. The news from the ghetto was bad, and I had some frightening experiences when I went out in the city. To come home to her twittering was more than I could bear. I was about ready to murder this sweet, innocent fool.

The Boys in the Streetcar

I HAD A BAD SCARE about two weeks before Easter. There was not much in the occupied city to remind people of the holidays. They had no money for shopping, and there was little to buy, anyway. But I knew Easter was approaching because Aunt Aniela was all excited and wanted me, her dear niece, to go with her to confession. I didn't know how I was going to wriggle out of that, but I was learning to think only from one day to the next. The day after tomorrow might never come.

I was in constant touch with the ghetto. My friend Rachel, who had escaped to the cellar with the Reichs and me, returned to work at the Judenrat switchboard as a messenger, running back and forth between the German authorities and the Jewish officials. She was also—illegally, of course—liaison between the ghetto and the outside world. The operator would say "Wrong number" if informers or troublemakers were present when such calls came in—a signal to wait until the coast was clear and try again.

Rachel was only sixteen, but very mature; young Jews had to grow up fast. She had lost her parents in the first deportation; now she was taking care of her little brother. She was fair-haired and blue-eyed, but he had "bad" looks—black hair, brown eyes, and a dark complexion. Since she had no money to pay for a hiding place for him, she had decided to stay in the ghetto.

I used to call her three or four times a week. This time Rachel asked me to meet Ida, who was ready to leave the ghetto. She had sent some money ahead for a shelter on the Aryan side, but she did not know the city and was afraid to ask directions on the street. I was to accompany her to her hiding place.

I was on time to meet Ida at the streetcar stop at the corner of Wilcza and Marszałkowska in downtown Warsaw. A few minutes later I saw her in the distance, and my heart stopped beating. She was rushing in my direction, surrounded by six boys of twelve or thirteen. These gangs of young blackmailers were very common. She should have pretended not to recognize me: the rule was not to endanger another when you yourself were threatened. A chased animal, she had lost her head. No one could doubt that she was Jewish and had just left the ghetto. She had failed the hardest test—the first hours on the Aryan side. She approached me, the boys stopping about two yards from us.

"What am I to do? Do I pay?"

This she should never have done in such an open place. Nor could she go anywhere near her new home. Once a blackmailer discovered where a Jew lived, he would come again and again, extorting everything his victim owned. Then sometimes he would hand him over to the Germans anyway and receive, in addition, a reward of 500 zlotys.

"Get on the streetcar," I whispered. "Don't let them go home with you. Tomorrow at the same place."

The streetcar arrived. She boarded it; the boys followed. But not all of them—three stayed with me. As I stood at the stop they eyed me arrogantly, saying not a word, probably glad to find such easy prey. "Stop looking at me!" I felt like shouting. Now I was in Ida's situation, but I could not pay them the money they would demand.

I could not go home either. They would have followed me. To gain time I took the first streetcar that came along. I found a place at the front and tried to maintain my air of cheerful self-possession. The three sat down in the middle of the car. They didn't dare start their game yet. Too many witnesses. Blackmailing was severely punished by the Germans; the Pole who recognized a Jew was supposed to notify them or the Polish police. But that was exactly what these boys did not want to do. Not yet. They probably expected to squeeze some money out of me and then claim the reward.

The three were in an excellent mood, talking and laughing. My situation seemed hopeless. They knew there could be no escape, since I would have to leave the car before the eight o'clock curfew. They were enjoying the war of nerves I could not win. We came to the last stop. I paid another fare. So did they. And a third time, same procedure. One after another, the other passengers left the car, hurrying home. Finally there were only the boys, the driver, and the conductor.

It was very late. Something had to be done. I looked at the conductor. My instinct told me I could trust him. To be deeply suspicious and yet capable of trusting was one of the secrets of survival. I had nothing to lose. I made up my mind.

"Those are blackmailers," I whispered to the conductor.

"Stay in the car. I will get rid of them."

"What about the curfew?" I asked him.

"If it's too late, you come back to my house. I have a night pass."

"Get off!" he ordered the boys.

This was unexpected. They had been outwitted and they lost their nerve. They knew they couldn't stay. They got up slowly.

One of them objected. "We paid the fare. We have a right . . ."

"Get off," the conductor repeated.

"What about this lady?" another boy tried again.

"None of your business."

Then the conductor called to the driver to stop. The driver braked sharply and my persecutors left. I had been saved.

A few minutes later, when I got up to leave the streetcar, all I could say was "Thank you, I have time to get home." We shook hands and I left. As long as I was in danger I had remained perfectly calm, as though my life had not been at stake. I felt detached from myself, as if I were playing a game. Self-control was a necessity; sometimes it could be more important for survival than money or an

Aryan appearance. But once the crisis was over, I was utterly exhausted. My head empty, my body trembling, I arrived home five minutes before curfew.

Miss Aniela awaited me as always, impatient to start her prattling. I could not bear it. Neither could I tell her I had a headache or felt very nervous; I was supposed to be cheerful. The danger was over for now, but I couldn't afford any more trouble. At that moment I hated her.

I solved the problem by telling her I was sleepy, but I could not sleep, wondering what was happening to Ida.

She did not show up the next day. She never reached her shelter. Nobody saw her again or knew what happened in what were probably her last hours.

Everything Breaks Down

DURING THOSE FIRST WEEKS in the Aryan part of Warsaw I lived in two different worlds. My mind and emotions remained in the ghetto, while my body explored the Polish city. These apparently quiet, safe, and unrestricted streets seemed to give the lie to what was going on behind the walls. The cleanliness and the spaciousness of the sidewalks still amazed me. Or at least they seemed spacious compared to the teeming passages in the ghetto, where one tried to avoid contact with others so as not to catch lice. There, walking skeletons dressed in rags crept from building to building. Sooner or later these specters would be found on the sidewalks covered with newspapers. They would be collected by Pinkiert's, the thriving firm of undertakers, and buried in common graves.

It was odd to see people smiling. In the ghetto, smiles

had vanished; the faces were worried or empty. Here people looked normal, yet to me they seemed unreal. Of course, Warsaw was nothing like its prewar self, when it was full of neon lights inviting people to movies, theaters, and restaurants. Still, this gray city in 1943 was a paradise after the ghetto. But I did not enjoy walking endlessly along streets where I saw not a single friendly soul. I was an exile, cut off from what had become my home, and from the people I loved.

Before I left the ghetto, I had been given messages from my Jewish friends for Poles they had known on the outside. Some asked for refuge; others asked me to make tactful inquiries about property left in their care. Some of these Poles refused to see me once they learned who had sent me. Others told me to call later but never found time for me. Some, embarrassed to refuse outright, tried to save face by meeting me to explain why they couldn't help. Nobody asked how I had managed to get settled on the Aryan side. It was not their affair.

There were a few real offers of help. I rushed to notify Rachel at the switchboard and she conveyed my messages to the interested parties. Unexpectedly, difficulties often arose on the Jewish side, as people postponed their departure to gain more time to smuggle out their belongings. Damned belongings! So many people perished because of them; the human lust for possessions prevailed over the instinct for life. In one case, negotiations were protracted because the Jewish family could not come to terms over the price of the shelter. Nobody could blame them for bargaining; either they lacked the money to accept this particular offer or they were afraid that what they had would not last them through the war. I returned to the

Poles with the new offer, and relayed the response to the Jews. In the end, the negotiations broke down.

I devoted much time and effort to an assignment I received from Szymon Majufes, a printer and a member of the Jewish Fighters' Organization (ŻOB). He asked me to find out if the People's Guard would accept a group of young ghetto volunteers who wanted to join the partisans in the woods.* Most Jews believed that the People's Guard was more sympathetic to them than the Home Army (Armia Krajowa), the military forces of the London-based Polish government-in-exile.

I followed Majufes's advice and went to see Hania Lanota and Eva Górska, both members of the Workers' Party. We had been schoolmates back in Lodz, and I knew their true names—Hania Rabinowicz and Sewa Prywes. They had a press in the basement of a little house in Mokotów, a suburb, where they printed an underground weekly, *The Voice of Warsaw*. They were friendly and promised to contact the People's Guard as soon as they could. Negotiations took longer than I expected—I assumed because of the great difficulty in arranging the escape of a considerable number of Jews to the woods. But that was not the only reason. I learned later that the People's Guard was reluctant to include Jews in its ranks, even though it needed new members.

Hania's husband, Edward Lanota, a People's Guard leader and himself a Jew, helped to overcome this anti-

---

* The People's Guard was the underground military arm of the Polish Workers' Party. The party, created in January 1942, was the successor to the former Communist Party of Poland, which had been dissolved by the Third International. The People's Guard was organized in June 1942 and became known as the People's Army in 1944.

Semitic bias. Later, during the Warsaw uprising, Lanota was the commandant of the People's Army and was killed along with all his officers. After the war, he became a national hero, yet none of the numerous publications devoted to the anti-Nazi activities of the Communist Party mentioned his Jewish origin or, rarely, the fact that many Jews fought and died in its military forces.

Finally Hania told me that the People's Guard had accepted the volunteers and that a representative would discuss the details with their prospective leader, Stefan Berman. Rachel passed along to Berman the time and the place, a bar in the city.

I knew Stefan Berman. Shortly before I left the ghetto I had met him at Majufes's place on the day after his bride of a few weeks had been sent to a death camp. He was brave and concealed his pain, talking mainly about plans for the young volunteers. I was proud now to have a share in this project; it added a new meaning to my decision to leave the ghetto. Stefan seemed to me an ideal choice for the assignment: resolute, courageous, competent. I liked him very much and I felt he liked me. At my one and only meeting with him I had been full of dreams about the future. Like others on the verge of the catastrophe, I would move quickly from desperation to hope and back down to sadness. When I said "See you soon" to Stefan, I had meant it. I already pictured him at my side, the charming and faithful friend I needed so much in my exile.

The mission failed. Stefan arrived on time, but when he entered the bar he did not notice that a roundup was going on: the police were searching for dealers in hard currency. Since Stefan had no Polish identification papers, he was arrested. The People's Guard representative was watching from outside the bar and saw what took place there. But we never learned exactly what happened at the police station. Evidently Stefan betrayed an address that I had conveyed to him through Rachel, that of an apartment rented to Hania in case the house with the basement press was discovered; the day after his arrest, police searched the apartment and sealed the door. We never learned whether Stefan betrayed the only address he knew because he had been beaten beyond endurance at the precinct or whether that was the price he had to pay for returning to the ghetto instead of being sent to prison or a concentration camp.

Since I had vouched for Stefan's courage and reliability, I expected that Hania would be very angry with me. She was understanding, but the subject of the Jewish group never came up again. I later learned from Rachel that Stefan had indeed returned safely to the ghetto, but she gave me no details. I never heard of him again.

My last mission was to rescue some relatives of mine: Dr. Zyf, a cousin; his wife, Dorka; and their five-year-old daughter, Stefcia. The prospects were very good. They did not look Jewish, their Polish was impeccable, and they had the money to stay on the Aryan side. I found what seemed an ideal shelter, a villa in Radość, a small village not far from Warsaw. The owner, a Polish Army officer, had been killed in the campaign of September 1939, and his widow agreed to take in the Zyfs for a moderate price. However, the Zyfs, who had urged me to find the place, were still not ready to leave. In the ghetto condemned to obliteration, people still looked for medical help, and while the Zyfs weren't greedy, the temptation to make more money prevailed. Every time I called Rachel I was told they would give me the exact day of their escape later. I was to call on April 20. On April 19, the uprising in the ghetto began.

It was the 14th day of Nisan, the first night of Passover, but I did not know that. Who could have told me when I was a Pole living among Poles? I can't recall how I learned that the uprising had begun. Was I told that German, Ukrainian, and Lithuanian troops and the Polish police had surrounded the walls the day before? Or had the news reached me the next day with the sound of the cannonade coming from the north? By the fifth day black clouds from the burning buildings hung over the entire city. All Warsaw knew that the last chapter of the ghetto's history was being written.

On the 20th, the second day, I called the switchboard, though I knew it was too late for my cousins; there was no escape for anyone. It was improbable that I could reach the besieged city. Yet, against all reason, I dialed the number. I can't remember whether the phone just kept ringing or a man's voice finally said there was no Rachel there.

The treachery of my memory upsets me, though this detail is no longer important. That the Germans were destroying the ghetto did not surprise me; it was predictable, certainly, after the January deportations. But it is one thing to anticipate a catastrophe, another to face up to it. And there is an unbridgeable gulf between knowledge and direct experience. It is strange, but only now do I really believe that my own parents died in the gas chambers. As I see on television the silent crowds being driven to their deaths, my imagination refuses to believe that they were in one of those columns. For many years I have waited for a sign from them—a letter gone astray, a stranger bearing news, a phone call from someone who saw them. I could not believe, because I was not there.

But the death of the ghetto I witnessed myself, albeit from the outside. Twice I approached the neighboring streets, knowing that they were very dangerous: German patrols scrutinized people's faces and blackmailers were on the lookout for recent fugitives. But many Jews living on the Aryan side had an overwhelming need to stay close to the perishing ghetto and to share its agony. Walking near the walls, I tried to read the faces of passersby. How did they feel about the tragedy they were witnessing? At first it seemed to me that they showed tension, fear, pain, and sympathy for the fighting and dying Jews. When next I looked, they seemed only curious or indifferent. I thought I heard words of sorrow and compassion. Maybe I saw and heard what I wanted to see and hear; perhaps I have erased other facts from my memory—the ones I wanted to forget. In order to survive, I had to believe that man is good.

I have gone back to those days so often that I can hardly distinguish among the sources of my knowledge of the events—what I witnessed myself, what I have been told by other people, what I have read in books. But my memory and my own experience have probably faded, given the total catastrophe. What did other witnesses have to say about the response of the Poles?

After the war, when the memory of the events was still fresh and the censors of the young Polish Communist state did not know exactly how to deal with the "Jewish question," there was some margin of freedom of expression. And among those who strongly rebuked the behavior of the Polish people were those Poles who had distinguished themselves in active support of the persecuted Jews—the noblest, the most courageous, the most generous of their countrymen. Here are the voices of Polish writers heard after the war.*

> *They turned away, their heads bowed, silent, or complaining that the world was evil and cruel, but giving thanks, deep in their hearts, for their own safety . . . And there were also those poisoned by the Nazi propaganda. These had the best of it, indeed. It's hard to believe but true . . . On Plac Krasińskich in the thick smoke of the nearby burning buildings the carousels turned round and round, the crowds overflowing.*
>
> —JANUSZ STĘPOWSKI

> *But the mood [of sympathy] changed before long. The indifferent majority, the average citizen, and the so-called intelligentsia began to complain about discomfort: about the black clouds of smoke, still billowing, spreading over Warsaw and literally blocking out the sun, choking the breath; about the unceasing cannonade of rifles, machine guns, artillery; and about growing transportation difficulties.* —SZCZĘSNY DOBROWOLSKI

As always in situations that are tragic for some, others knew how to profit. There were the blackmailers, the informers, and the looters of "post-Jewish property" left behind by the Jews. Since the Germans had cut off many streetcars to isolate the ghetto, a new kind of enterprise sprang up—scores of carts and other horse-drawn vehicles, charging for a distance of three streetcar stops what it normally cost for fifteen. "In spite of this, business thrived," remarked Adolf Rudnicki, a novelist who wrote a number of books on the Holocaust.

---

* These quotations are taken from Joseph Kermish, *The Warsaw Ghetto Uprising* (Lodz: Central Jewish Historical Committee, 1946). Szczęsny Dobrowolski, Stefa's husband, had helped me escape from the ghetto.

Rudnicki describes the non-stop processions to the ghetto walls throughout Holy Week:

> *The crowds flowed out of the churches, still fervently spiritual
> . . . carrying flowers. They walked toward the walls, toward the
> spectacle—the Warsaw Paschal spectacle.*
>   *They came and went. They looked, said they were sorry. They
> were sorry about the goods, the riches, the gold, the fabulous gold,
> but most of all they were sorry about the apartments and the
> buildings, the most beautiful buildings. They said "Couldn't
> King Hitler have solved this problem in a different way?" The
> glow of the fire could be seen from any corner of Warsaw. About
> all this, about the children burned alive, this is what they said:
> "It's in the ghetto," and then they regained peace of mind. The
> ghetto was burning and people said, "How lucky we are there's
> no wind. Otherwise, our buildings could also burn" . . . One
> could also hear: "It's good that we didn't have to do it."*

Jerzy Andrzejewski, a brilliant writer, said in his novel *The Night (Noc)*: "To the man in the street, the very need to fight a handful of lonely Jews made the victorious occupier look foolish." Some people believed that the Nazis' obsession with the Jews would deflect their hostility toward the Poles; others warned, "First the Jews. We are next." Some sources say the ghetto received all the assistance possible under the circumstances; others question this. Every political faction claimed credit for supporting the fighters. There were genuine acts of heroism, but nobody, on either side, could deny that the help given was minimal. The facts remain to be investigated. Western historians have estimated that the Home Army and the People's Guard conducted no more than a dozen forays in and around the ghetto.

How very true and how very sad are the words of Janusz Korczak, the great writer and teacher who accompanied the children of his orphanage to their death: "Nothing is easier to get used to than the misfortune of others."

I Make Friends

It was late May 1943. The sun was high and bright, the air fresh. Occasionally a breeze would carry fumes from the still smoldering ruins of what had recently been a city and was now an immense field of ashes and debris. Silence hung over the area. Warsaw began to breathe freely; those who had felt compassion relaxed. How long can one feel compassion? Those who had celebrated the end of the ghetto found other entertainment, such as hunting the few Jews who had escaped death. How long could they celebrate a spectacle that was over? And strangely enough, we Jews who were pretending to be Polish began to live our normal lives, or what passed for normal lives. We enjoyed having a place to live as long as it remained a refuge; we relished every minute of safety; we felt the sun's warmth with pleasure and admired the flowering fruit trees. Every day that passed without trouble was a gift. A sparkle of beauty or joy made the shortest moment immensely precious. Crossing the Prince Poniatowski Bridge in Warsaw and looking at the Vistula in the light of sunset, I would feel that seeing the river once more justified my struggle to endure; I even dared to hope that the next day might bring something good.

And something good happened: I made some friends. I was no longer alone, could talk openly, be myself, trust someone else. No friendship can compare with those put to the test in wartime. What happened to my friends happened to me. Their stories became my own.

I heard someone calling my name one day as I walked aimlessly down Marszałkowska Street. Almost before I recognized Marysia, I was in her arms. We had not met for many years and had never been close, but we were both very happy to see each other. Some Jews pretended not to recognize old acquaintances, Jewish as well as Polish: anyone could be a blackmailer. But Marysia and I were not afraid of people who were in the same predicament. She invited me on the spot to the apartment where she was nursing an elderly Polish countess in return for room, board, and a small salary—an excellent arrangement for the times. Marysia was a sweet girl, patient and reliable. Her patient's son, the count, realized what a treasure she was. Sometimes we wondered if he ever suspected she was Jewish. If he did, he never revealed it.

His housekeeper, however, presented some danger to Marysia. Once she insisted that Marysia wash the old lady's sheets, although the laundry was one of her own duties. It seemed a trivial matter, but not under those circumstances; she would never have asked a nurse to do this work if she had not suspected something. Not that she wanted to denounce her; she simply saw the chance to rid herself of a chore and at the same time gain some power over Marysia. "The neighbors say that Miss Marysia is Jewish," she remarked. "They may be right."

Although it was dangerous to antagonize her, Marysia refused to do the laundry. To give in would mean that she was afraid of the woman. She decided to complain to the count, who ordered the housekeeper to attend to her usual duties.

The count treated his mother's nurse with respect. I guessed that he was not interested in women; in any case, Marysia did not have to concern herself with the extraneous demands sometimes made in such households. But her patient was a heavy woman, and the work was sometimes tiring. When the count proposed that I relieve Marysia on weekends, I agreed. Luckily she could stay with Polish friends, whom she referred to as her family. When I was on duty, the countess would call every half hour, "Miss Irene, please, the bedpan!" Irene had been the name of a former nurse, and now I was Irene XV or XVI. I didn't mind.

In the morning, breakfast was served to the count and me. We would sit in the large dining room, under the portraits of his ancestors. There was hot cereal with milk, cheese, excellent rolls, jam, and real coffee—for me, a Lucullan meal. My aristocratic host, always meticulously dressed, had a narrow face with a perpetually sarcastic look. But he was unfailingly polite, and felt it his duty to entertain me during the meal. Before the war he had been attached to the Polish Embassy in Moscow, and he liked to talk about Russia. He was strongly anti-Russian, whereas

I was a socialist and—like all Jews then—expected the Russians to deliver us. Obviously, under the circumstances, I couldn't speak my mind, so I would listen in a ladylike manner. He was intelligent and well informed. This I admit now. But then I considered him a reactionary and it was painful to have to swallow my opinions, though I managed never to say anything contrary to my beliefs.

My visits with Marysia were a source of warmth and comfort to me. The housekeeper, who liked me very much, used to treat me to her excellent potato blintzes and other specialties. For me any food was delicious and special; it was a welcome addition to my poor diet.

Shortly after I met Marysia, I came to know Celinka. I wondered why she never removed the scarf she wore on her head. Later she explained that she had gone to a hairdresser to have her dark hair bleached. When she came out from under the dryer, she was almost bald; doubtless, the hairdresser had used cheap chemicals. A Gentile customer would have reacted violently and certainly claimed damages, but a Jewish client couldn't afford to attract attention. So Celinka hadn't protested, had even paid the man for his "services." Now she was concerned that the scarf might make her look more Jewish.

Celinka's war experiences had been harsher than mine. She had left Warsaw in 1939 and gone to Lvov, then occupied by the Russians. There she continued the medical studies she had begun before the war, and received her degree in the spring of 1941. When the Russian–German war broke out, she could have been evacuated to Russia, but she decided to return to Warsaw to join her widowed mother. Her brother, a lawyer who had joined the Polish Army, was killed in September 1939. An older sister, an outstanding mathematician, was murdered by the Nazis when they entered Bialystok in June 1941. Celinka felt it her duty to be with her mother.

Celinka and her mother escaped from the ghetto in 1942. Their first refuge was with Alek Milecki, Celinka's fellow medical student. Their stay was brief, like mine at Miss Okonska's, and for a similar reason. Other Jewish lodgers turned up who were better off than they were. Although Alek asked no rent of his Jewish friends, it was more profitable to keep the new lodgers because he was in the business of forging papers and they recommended him to rich clients from the ghetto. Alek, of course, tried to justify his decision, I forget how. Excuses could always be found. Celinka didn't reproach him; she preferred to part friends. In another crisis he might be helpful. No mention was made, either, of the fur coat her mother had left for safekeeping with Alek. All winter it had been worn by his wife, while the mother wore a light summer coat. Most likely, had she asked for it back, Alek would have returned it. She did not ask; for Jews, it was often smarter to lose. But Celinka deeply resented such a situation, more than the rest of us did. She had great integrity and never indulged herself or others. Yet she had to compromise. After the war she was to become stubborn, rigid, intolerant. I thought I knew why.

When I think about Alek's conduct, I believe it shouldn't obscure his undeniable merits. He was courageous, often generous, and endangered himself and his family by helping the Jews. Yet his decency remained in question. People's psyches were damaged then, sometimes irreversibly. Among Poles and Jews alike, the law of the stronger not only justified crimes but created an atmosphere in which corruption flourished among otherwise decent and honest people.

Celinka and her mother moved often after they left Alek's. The mother, a capable and dignified woman, was able to get work as a housekeeper for affluent Polish families. She was always treated with respect, even though housekeepers were considered servants. With her small salary and the leftovers from her employer's table, she helped Celinka to survive.

Celinka was often out looking for a job or a new shelter. Once she came up against a blackmailer who dragged her into an abandoned building and raped her. Later she encountered him again. This time she escaped to the top floor of the nearest building, climbed out on a window ledge, and told the blackmailer she would jump if he came near her. She meant it. The man saw she was serious; he wanted her living body, not her corpse. For a while he hung around, then left. Celinka dreaded meeting him again. The ordeal haunted her for a long time.

When I met her, she had just found a room in a large apartment next door to one occupied by two young Jews. They guessed that she was Jewish and did not hesitate to warn the landlady; again, Jews did not want other Jews in the same shelter. The landlady ignored them, and Celinka moved in.

Celinka learned this from the landlady, much later. Yet the young men were good people, and we all became very friendly. After the war, one became a writer, the other a well-known movie director. Neither during the war nor afterward did I remind them that they had tried to keep Celinka from moving into the apartment. Had I mentioned it, they certainly would not have admitted it. They might have claimed that the landlady invented the story to test Celinka. Or they might have had no memory of the episode. People tend to brush away memories that reflect unfavorably on their character.

Miss Okonska and the girls who caused me to leave her apartment, Alek who took Celinka's mother's fur coat, the young men who tried to keep Celinka out of their shelter—all these individuals set aside moral principle. I wonder if they were immoral or merely pitiable; if these lapses—one could say minor occurrences—should be extricated from the subconscious or simply overlooked. I cannot forget them. I remember too well those who maintained the highest standards and some who paid for their integrity with their lives.

Celinka and I often shared our food. Bread was a luxury. We used to cook a porridge of millet that before the war had been fed to chickens; sometimes it burned because we had no fat. But nothing could spoil our pleasure. Celinka would try to convince me that she wasn't very hungry and would give me the larger share. I tried to do the same. Now it seems to me that she was somehow the stronger one, and I the one more easily convinced. Did she really require less food than I? Or did she know how to hide her own hunger so that I would take more? Such behavior was exceptional. I recall a married couple, very respectable people, who used to weigh their bread to be sure each had exactly half the ration. Celinka would never do that. Her magnanimity could be understood only by those who had themselves once starved.

I was running out of the little money I had. Mrs. Uklejska, my old headmistress, was concerned. She was unable to find me a tutoring job in the underground education system, but it occurred to her that I could teach book-keeping to her daughter Maria. I had a business-school diploma, but I doubted that Maria, a former art student, really needed my help. But Mrs. Uklejska, skilled in the art of persuasion, convinced me that Maria, who was working in her father's factory, had to learn bookkeeping, and I took the job.

When I dropped in for tea at Mrs. Uklejska's, I felt transported to another planet. She had a way of conferring favors on me and making me feel that I was the benefactor. I would ring their bell and whoever came to the door—my headmistress or one of her daughters—would call out to the others, "Zofia is here!" This excited welcome, which might seem gushing and insincere in others, came naturally to them. What a contrast to the reception given most ghetto refugees by their former Polish friends! People were afraid that they might be asked for a favor. Sometimes they were embarrassed, because the Jewish person who appeared in their homes as a miserable hunted creature was once highly respected or even someone to whom they were indebted. Even if they attempted to conceal their embarrassment, the Jewish visitor, particularly sensitive and vulnerable, would be aware of the hosts' true feelings.

Mrs. Uklejska, in her late forties, her dark hair graying, still wore the tailored suits and the glasses on a chain that I remembered from my school days. She was a gracious hostess, as befitted her upbringing in an aristocratic family, and presided over the tea table as if the war had never existed and the pastries were not made with ersatz ingredients. We laughed a lot. Only there, in those little "seminars," did I have a chance to exchange ideas.

One afternoon I felt I had to tell her that I was a socialist, that she was helping a political adversary. (She was a conservative in politics.) She told me, laughing, that she had known this years before, when I was a student. She had given me a hint when I was taking my final oral examination, just before I left the Gymnasium. I had quoted from Julian Tuwim's "The White House," a poem about workers who wanted to build a house of a hundred thousand stories to reach the sky. "Doesn't it remind you of Russian workers, with their Stakhanovite ideas?" she had asked me, referring to the Soviet hero of production. "I think you're familiar with the concept." I had replied that I was, but I didn't realize then that she was signaling to me that she had guessed my politics but would not betray me. If my opinions had become known, there might have been a move to expel me. "Your politics had nothing to do with our friendship then," she told me, "and they have nothing to do with our friendship now."

All my life, Maria Uklejska has remained for me the model of tolerance and understanding.

How to Become a Legal Pole

M<small>Y ONLY IDENTIFICATION</small> thus far was a birth certificate issued in the name of Zofia Sielczak. It was not enough. Everyone under the occupation had to have a Kennkarte indicating name, date and place of birth, present occupation, and religion.

Under the Nazis, many people used counterfeit documents. The forging of papers flourished, not only for Jews, but for former officers of the Polish Army, high officials of the prewar Polish government, politicians, intellectuals who had engaged in anti-Nazi activities, and those in the underground. But after the deportations from the ghetto began, the clientele was largely Jewish. Some counterfeiters were themselves in the underground and rendered their services for very little or for free. But most found it a profitable business. The quality of the forged documents varied according to price and the craftsman's skill and honesty. An ID filled in on a blank Kennkarte was relatively cheap: it could easily be exposed, since there were no corresponding records in the official files.

Poles obtained true IDs by submitting a birth certificate to the office that issued the Kennkarte. Birth certificates were issued by the Church. However, there were "good" and "bad" birth certificates. The latter were those filled out with fictitious data on blank birth-certificate forms. The good ones were "authentic"—that is, they had been issued to real persons who had left the country or had died. Sometimes the forger did not receive an original certificate from the Church but was permitted to copy data from the certificate of a deceased or absent person. In such cases, to avoid duplication, the clerk or priest had to make a note of the transaction. My certificate was one copied in this manner from the Church files.

I decided to act like a true Pole and obtain an "authentic" Kennkarte. This meant going in person to the city office and submitting my photograph and my "birth certificate." It involved some risk but had the advantage of providing me with an original document. I was edgy under the photographer's lights, thinking that the man had an excellent opportunity to study my face and realize that I was Jewish. But nothing like that happened. Everything at the Stadthauptmann's office went smoothly, too. I submitted my picture and the birth certificate; they took my fingerprints and I received my Kennkarte. It would expire May 8, 1948. The Germans were optimistic about their future in Poland.

The next step for me as a true Pole was to register my address with the vital-records office. Everything seemed perfect, but it was not. I could not have foreseen that there were two false Zofia Sielczaks born of the same parents on the same date. Another forger had copied the same certificate, because a careless priest or clerk had not checked it off as already copied. Somewhere in Warsaw there was another woman with the identical birth certificate who had followed the same procedure and registered *her* address with the vital-records office. When that happened, the office took action, as I was soon to learn.

Goodbye, Aunt Aniela

IT WAS AROUND NOON when I came home to rest awhile. I noticed immediately that the usually serene Aunt Aniela was very nervous. Before I could take off my coat, she blurted out: "About an hour ago a policeman was here asking for you. He said there were two persons by the name of Zofia Sielczak, both born on the same day and with the same parents. One or both must be Jewish."

I tried to laugh. "That's funny," I said. "Just imagine: another girl with my name!"

Now I was the one who prattled.

Aunt Aniela was not amused. "I assured him that you are not Jewish, that you are a good Catholic girl. Of course you are."

I saw that the poor thing badly wanted to convince herself as well as the policeman.

"He said that it was his duty to come back and talk to you. He will be back in a little while."

I did my best to persuade Aunt Aniela that there must be some misunderstanding; I would explain it to the policeman.

"Dear child, if you are Polish and Catholic, stay with me. I love you like my own daughter. But if you are Jewish—run away! He will come back and arrest you. May God Almighty bless you and keep you in His mercy!"

For a moment she was silent. Then solemnly she made the sign of the cross over my head. On her otherwise ordinary face there appeared an expression of nobility. I looked around for the last time, my eyes resting on the cheap, unframed pictures of the *other* saints in the room. I pitied her and tried to cheer her up. I assured her that I was the good Catholic girl she knew, that I would stay with her. I had to go out again, I said, but I would be back in an hour.

"See you soon, Aunt Aniela!"

I never saw her again. She must be long dead. Sometimes I am obsessed by the thought that I am perhaps the only person who remembers her. May she rest in peace.

I left the apartment and walked fast to escape from the policeman, who might be following me. It ran through my head that the other Zofia, my double, was in the same fix. I guessed what had happened; I knew how forgers operated. I was lucky to get out before the policeman returned, but I didn't know where to go. I rapidly reviewed the short list of my friends and acquaintances in Warsaw, something I had to do often. I had to be prepared for a crisis at any time. Now I think about those friends with some embarrassment: I was always considering how useful they might be to me. Yet I think I am not a person who is prone to take advantage of others.

No one on my list was in a position to help me. It was a consolation that Mrs. Uklejska or Marysia could put me up for a night or two—but no longer; and even that might endanger them. I had to find a shelter right away. My thoughts were scattered. Suddenly, as in the flash of a camera, the room where I had lived in my Gymnasium days came to my memory—much to my surprise, since I hadn't thought about it for a long time. It was a room in the apartment of a widow who took in lodgers for a living.

One of them was Nina Nieszawska, an orphan who lived with her aunt while going to business school. She was very popular, and her aunt wouldn't let her go out with men, but trusted me. I regret to say that I betrayed her confidence. Nina and I would leave the apartment together, ostensibly to go to the movies, but we would separate at the corner and Nina would join one of her boyfriends. Later we would meet in front of the house and return together. Everyone was pleased with this arrangement.

Nina was Jewish, and I had no idea what had happened to her. But I remembered meeting a couple of her Polish boyfriends. There was a wild chance that they might be in the city. Fantastic as it seems—I scarcely knew them—I decided to try to find them.

Both Filip Panicek and Janek Nowak were listed in the telephone directory I consulted in a café. I tried Panicek first, at his camera store. His pleasant, boyish face showed real surprise when I walked in: Jews were supposed to be dead or in concentration camps, not walking around on the Aryan side. I explained why I'd come. He was very frank. He told me that since he was of Czech origin, born in the Sudetenland (which the Nazis considered part of Germany), he had applied for Folksdeutsch (ethnic German) status. He had German customers who sometimes visited him at home, and couldn't risk helping me.

I left thinking things could be worse: a Folksdeutsch was supposed to denounce Jews. But I didn't think Panicek would betray me. I was learning to be grateful to people not only for what they did for me but also for what they didn't do against me.

Twenty minutes later I knocked at the door of the house where Janek Nowak lived with his parents. He opened it—a sturdy, rather bluff young man. He seemed frightened to see me but he was friendly, and I felt better. I couldn't stay there, he said. His parents were sympathetic to Jews but would not endanger themselves. However, he had a girlfriend, Danka Dunin, who lived in the country, in Zbójna Góra, about thirty miles from Warsaw. Perhaps she would take me in. She lived alone in a villa that belonged to a Folksdeutsch, the boss of the city sanitation department where Janek and Danka both worked. Danka lived there rent-free as caretaker. The owner rarely showed up.

I waited while Janek picked up Danka at work, so that he could sound her out about me. Then I met them both at the railroad station, as arranged. Danka was slender and very pretty; she had dark, curly hair and lively brown eyes. I thought that she could have been charming if she had wanted to be, but now she looked me up and down in a sharp, unpleasant way and said curtly, "She can come with me."

We took the train to Radość and walked two miles on

sandy ground to Zbójna Góra. The name of this hamlet means Bandit's Mountain in Polish, but it looked lovely and peaceful. The house stood at the edge of a deep wood. There was only one other building in sight, across a country road. It seemed an ideal haven.

Sweet, Quiet Countryside

MY FIRST NIGHT with Danka passed quietly, without much conversation. Perhaps Danka was reconsidering her decision to take me in. Perhaps she was tired. In any case, she asked no questions, and I was grateful for that. I was exhausted. I thought about the way chance had rescued me all afternoon. If I had gone back to Aunt Aniela's half an hour earlier or had left there half an hour later, I might have been arrested and handed over to the Gestapo. If I had not called up Janek Nowak, a casual acquaintance from the past . . . If he had been unwilling to help me . . . If this girl had refused to accept a total stranger . . .

Next morning, as Danka left for her job, she asked me if I had any reason to go to Warsaw. Fortunately, I did not. My bookkeeping lessons for Mrs. Uklejska's daughter and some tutoring in Latin for a high school student in the underground educational system were scheduled for the following week, and I could stay in the country and rest.

As soon as I was alone, I toured the house. There was a big living room downstairs and three bedrooms and a bath upstairs—a striking contrast to the tiny room I had shared with Aunt Aniela. Best of all, I was in the country, for the first time in four years. The garden was not planted, but the grass and trees seemed the greenest I'd ever seen. The leaves sparkled, and the silence was broken only by birdsong. I opened the gate and in five minutes I was in the forest. I lay on the ground, taking in the smell of the earth and the shrubbery, looking at the sky through the tops of the trees. I should have been happy, but I was worried. If there is a form of meditation that detaches people from reality, I have never learned it. Now, in all this beauty, I kept thinking of Danka. What was she like? How would we get along? How long would I be safe? How soon would I need another shelter? I was restless. I wanted to do something for Danka, and the only thing that came to mind was cleaning the house. I thought that would please her, and I got up and hurried home.

I swept the floors and scrubbed the cupboards in the kitchen. I scoured the bathroom until it seemed spotless. Then I waited impatiently for the return of my hostess.

I heard the gate creak and there she was, holding in each hand a basket containing a few potatoes, some carrots and cabbage, and a pot of soup. Danka was a potato peeler at the sanitation-department employees' canteen; the women who worked there were entitled to a daily ration of soup and vegetables. Usually they stole an additional portion— some soup, a few extra vegetables.

"What did you do all day?" she asked.

"Don't you see? I cleaned," I answered proudly. I felt I had done a good job.

She glanced at the kitchen and set down her baskets but did not take off her coat. She kicked off her shoes. Long worn and probably too big, they landed in the middle of the kitchen. She snatched up a rag and began feverishly to dust the cupboards I had just cleaned. She had an air of super-efficiency and self-importance.

Without interrupting her cleaning, she said, "You should learn what hard work means . . . should use elbow grease." She wasn't just criticizing my work. She was belittling me.

I stood rooted to the spot. I had the urge to run away. This was more than I could take. She glanced at me, saw that I was stunned. She stopped scrubbing.

"Come, I brought some soup. Let's eat. It's late."

The laconic sentences and the rather embarrassed expression on her face showed me that I had met a kind of human being I had never encountered before—a mixture of the commonplace and the sensitive, the mean and the magnanimous. At supper Danka tried to make up for her earlier brusqueness, but she was awkward and didn't know how. She had not yet learned to express gradations of feeling and she didn't realize how deeply she had hurt me. I was very upset.

It was the fourth year of the war and I had encountered enough cruelty to toughen me for the harshest exchanges. Why was I so shocked by Danka's bluntness? I may have feared that she would throw me out, but that was not the reason. I was deeply insulted, my best intentions rejected. I had always been thin-skinned when people were rude.

Now, in spite of my narrow escapes, in spite of the constant threat of death, I was reacting as I would in normal circumstances. I have since realized that preserving one's self-respect, even one's sensitivity in small things, was an important source of strength when one was an outlaw and the object of persecution on an unprecedented scale.

At the time I didn't realize that Danka's outburst wasn't really aimed at me, that she had a kind of free-floating anger against everyone and everything—the result of a bitter life. In all our future relations there was never a recurrence of this kind of incident. I kept on cleaning, but she made no comments when she came home and she shared her food with me.

But after two weeks she said, "Zofia, you'd better stop doing the housework. Leave it to me. You'd better read, or rest, or whatever you want to do."

This was not a criticism, though I could not keep up with her work. It meant that our relations had entered a new stage: she found me a new kind of being, different from any she'd ever met. She thought I was "too good" for housekeeping, created for "higher things." Strangely enough, this inflated opinion of my virtues was strengthened by my being Jewish. At first her talk had been unsympathetic to the Jews in the way of rank-and-file Poles: Jews were cunning, insincere, selfish, greedy. But she had never been close to a Jew. Now, when she saw how different I was from the people she knew, she became convinced that Jews were superior. I could not change her mind. Later this conviction would alter the course of her entire life.

Her feeling for me was more than liking; it was a kind of passionate devotion, an intense love. We grew steadily closer, discovering each other's very different worlds. She began to see that there was more to life than brutality and harshness. A knowledge of her experiences is necessary for an understanding of mine. That is why I have to tell her story.

Danka's Story

DANKA WAS BORN and raised in Powiśle, a section of Warsaw that had once been the ancient bed of the Vistula. It lies at the bottom of a steep wooded slope that was a favorite haunt of lovers. Inhabited mainly by the poor, it was notorious for the pickpockets and other criminals who frequented its streets after dark.

Danka's mother disappeared soon after she was born, for reasons unknown to me. Danka lived with her father, and all I knew about him was that he had gone blind when she was a child and that her stepmother usually ended the daily fights at home by beating him up. After his death, Danka was brought up by this woman, if blows, screams, and curses may be so described. Yet her stepmother's behavior seemed almost natural to Danka; the woman treated her own son and daughter the same way. The daughter died of consumption when she was fifteen, and Danka lived with her stepmother and stepbrother in one room until the war broke out. The sanitation commissioner's villa near Radość, where we were living now, was the first place that Danka could call her own.

I met Danka's stepmother a number of times when I visited her with Danka. She was a malicious old woman with a twisted mouth and piercing eyes. Her voice was a screech. Maybe she wasn't as hateful as she looked to me. She abused the children? Everybody did. She had beaten her blind husband? Wasn't that what he deserved? Wasn't he another mouth to feed? Should she have petted him? Still, Danka visited her quite often and seemed grateful to her. Hadn't the old woman fed her when she was a child? Danka seldom went empty-handed, and after the war supported her as well as she could.

Danka was very pretty. Her small head was beautifully shaped; she would toss it to one side in a charming way, in the next minute throwing back her dark curly hair. Her vivid brown eyes were keen and bright. She was slim, of medium height, and moved gracefully. She was certainly very attractive, especially to men. She had only an elementary-school education, but she was intelligent and perceptive, quick to take her cue from more cultured company. She was silent when she was out of her depth, but she learned fast, asking the right questions and making good use of her newly acquired knowledge.

When she was sixteen or seventeen, she told me, she had met a young French diplomat who had fallen in love with her and wanted to marry her. My first reaction was to doubt this—her stories usually had to be taken with a grain of salt. But this one seemed to ring true. To run ahead of my story: In 1959, when I was in Paris, I found her admirer's number in the phone book. He lived in a fashionable neighborhood. His private secretary took my call and explained that his boss was very ill and found it too tiring to talk. He took my message—regards from Danka—and told me to hold on. Then someone else was on the line, the former lover's son. He said his father was paralyzed but wanted Danka to know that he was deeply touched to hear from her and that he preserved the warmest memories of her. So it did seem like a serious affair—rather like a movie in which the Cinderella from Powiśle married a distinguished member of the French diplomatic corps.

But Danka was not fated to live in wealth and happiness—or more accurately, it was not in her nature to make rational choices. While the young Frenchman was courting her, she had fallen in love with a captain of the Polish police. Bednarek—that was his name—had a wife and two daughters. I couldn't tell how genuine his feelings for Danka were. Maybe he loved her very much, as she insisted when she told me about him. Maybe an affair with a pretty girl so much younger than his wife was just an exciting adventure. However, there was no doubt that he did promise marriage to Danka. If he really intended to go through with this plan, it would have been extremely difficult to work things out in the Catholic Church, where obtaining a divorce was complicated, expensive, and in fact often impossible. Danka was working in a factory then—this was before the war—and she used to give Bednarek money from her small wages for the divorce. He took the money, but God knows how he spent it. Certainly not for the divorce. In rare moments of candor he would admit that he couldn't make up his mind because he loved his daughters so much and didn't want to hurt them. Also—unless I missed my guess—he was scared off by Danka's temperament, by the unrestrained passion with which she did everything. When she lost her temper, there were violent scenes in public. Danka admitted that Bednarek sometimes went for weeks trying to avoid her, but Danka was persistent. More than once she spent the night sitting on the police-station steps to waylay her lover. And when he arrived, she would beat him with the umbrella she had brought along for that purpose. I found it easy to imagine how he felt, held up to ridicule in front of his colleagues, and I could guess what the unfortunate lover would encounter when he got home to his wife.

Listening to these stories, and to others like them, I could not help laughing uproariously. Danka saw nothing funny in these situations, but later she got used to my very different sense of humor. I laughed, but at the same time I felt like crying. These things had happened in a world I had never known. Of course, I had read about such things in the Warsaw *Express*, an afternoon scandal sheet. But it had never occurred to me that I would actually come to know someone who acted out these dramas.

Danka showed me many photographs of Bednarek; I saw a handsome, intelligent face. He impressed me as a man of tough character and few scruples. Danka looked at the photographs—who knew how many times—with incredible fondness and pride. He was *the* lover. Usually Danka was a rather suspicious person. But when she fell for someone, she became naïve and immensely gullible. That is why Bednarek could take advantage of her so easily.

And so their stormy relationship lasted for years, until the war broke out. Then he disappeared.

Janek spent most of his time with Danka in the villa, but occasionally he went home to his parents in Warsaw, sometimes staying away for long periods. While he was gone, Danka and I would while away our evenings with stories about her past—most of all, stories about Bednarek. She talked about him so vividly and with such emotion that their affair could have been carried on yesterday. Sometimes I heard different versions of the same incident. What was curious was that Danka had no reason to lie. Maybe the different versions stemmed not from an inclination to lie but from an inability to tell the truth. If she said she paid less for something than she actually did pay, it was not because she wanted to boast that she was good at buying. If she said she paid more, it was not because she wanted to impress people with what she could afford. There was no rational explanation for her little lies. She would provide all sorts of trivial details—such as the date and the hour—that had no bearing on events. I came to notice similar embellishments among other people I met at this time, all of them from harsh backgrounds like Danka's. Perhaps they used these lies as a defense when they felt threatened in a hostile milieu.

At first, when I caught Danka in one of her little lies, I never failed to point it out. She didn't resent that. As a matter of fact, nothing I said offended her; I could say anything I wanted. She would laugh and admit that I was right; she seemed to realize how absurd her lies were. Yet she never got rid of the habit. For my part, I learned a lot in my friendship with Danka: to concentrate on the real values in a human being and to pay less attention to unconventional behavior.

I began to pretend not to notice her deviations from the truth when I saw that they raised her spirits and made her feel important. If she witnessed a fire or a car accident, she liked to say that it was a big fire or a tragic accident. Witnessing these events meant almost as much to her as participating in them. And an important event was somehow more "elegant" than a minor one; it gave meaning to the emptiness of her existence. In this way she became the heroine of a drama, if only for a short time.

Many years earlier, I had read Karel Čapek's short story "The Book for Servants," which discussed the importance of cheap romance novels for girls in domestic service—novels that raised the possibility that a miracle might befall these pitiable creatures, just as it had rescued the heroine of the wretched melodrama. So I let Danka dream that she was a Cinderella waiting for her prince.

Of course, there was nothing in Bednarek that resembled the fairy tale's gentle prince. And Danka's innocent dreams would turn out to have far-reaching consequences. When I listened to her stories, I did not want to deprive her of her illusions, because I thought that Bednarek's case was closed. Unfortunately, it was not.

One evening, Danka returned home very excited. Before she took off her coat and put away her baskets, she told me that she had heard news of Bednarek. Early in the war he had fled to Lvov; a friend had given her his address there. Danka was radiant; all the old stories took on a new life. I did not like it at all. I had a presentiment that Danka's very stability was threatened. I approved of her relationship with Janek. He was an honest man; he would give her a quiet, decent life after the war, I thought. Now the revival of the old dreams about Bednarek seemed to endanger the future. I told myself that Lvov was far away, that her excitement would wear off.

I was wrong. I didn't realize how strong her passion was, how persistent she could be. But I sensed that she was concocting something, and was not really surprised when a few days later, with the most innocent air in the world, she remarked, "You know, we could write a letter to Bednarek, just for fun."

I heard that "we." It was clear that I was to write the letter and she would put it in her own handwriting and sign it. I was dead-set against it, but she wouldn't listen to my objections. With tears in her eyes, she asked me to do it. If I refused, she would write it anyway, but she knew I would write it better. Couldn't I do it for her? Finally I gave in.

And so began our—Danka's and my—correspondence with Bednarek. He answered our first letter immediately. He was clearly pleased with Danka's letter, his male vanity touched by her constancy. Besides, he was impressed by the intellectual development so clearly demonstrated in the letter's form and content. I may say without false modesty that the letter was written with dignity, imagination, and humor. It was full of subtle allusions to their past. Danka, in raptures because I managed to express exactly what she wanted to convey to Bednarek, pressed me to reply promptly. I felt like the Madame Récamier of Radość as I practiced my epistolary arts. Soon I was drawn into the game, becoming more and more involved. Writing and reading these letters—Bednarek's were intelligent and witty—brightened our gray and hungry evenings. We had great fun. But I did not understand Danka well enough then. For her, this was much more than fun; it was the first of a number of serious steps she was soon to take.

Murder: Case Closed

NEVER HAD I FELT so close to nature as during that beautiful late spring of 1943 when I lived with Danka in Radość. The Jews who hid in the countryside during the German occupation often recollect how intensely they responded to the charms of fields, meadows, forests, rivers, mountains; how they enjoyed the changes in the light and the shifts of the wind.

In the ghetto we seldom saw plants and trees. The children couldn't imagine what a forest looked like; the spindly trees in the few squares of the ghetto did not help to create an image of woods. They never saw an ear of corn, rarely a flower. A child asked me once what a cow looked like. Almost all cats and dogs had been eaten. The only animals to be seen were the few horses harnessed to the ghetto streetcar operated by the firm of Kohn and Heller, two

Jewish Gestapo men. And those who lived on the Aryan side of Warsaw avoided the parks. Many left home only when it was necessary. Some, hiding in cellars or attics, did not see the sun for years. This is probably why the longing for nature was so strong among us, the hunted and persecuted. This is why, for me, this spring of 1943 in the country seemed a stay in paradise. After all my experiences, I felt that I had found the most beautiful place— and the safest shelter—on earth.

I went to Warsaw only a few days a week. I tried to do all my tutoring then so that I could spend the rest of the week in the country. I remained faithful to my plan to put down roots wherever I lived and to make new friends. Actually, though, there were few people around, most of them the tenants of the Baptist house across the road (so called because of the religious affiliation of the owners, so exotic in that setting). Soon I made friends with one of them, Lena, a pretty, elegant woman in her thirties. She lived with her five-year-old daughter, who was convalescing from some illness and needed fresh country air. Maybe there were other reasons for her to be in Radość. I did not know. Many people there had reasons for not disclosing their affairs. I never pried; certainly I had my own reasons for preferring not to be asked too many questions.

Lena did, however, volunteer some information about herself. She was separated from her husband; this explained the frequent visits of a handsome young man, Tadeusz Malinowski. After we became closer, she confided in me that Tadeusz was a Folksdeutsch; he was a very honest man, she said, and a good patriot, but for some reason felt compelled to declare his German extraction.

I used to meet Lena quite often. I liked her—she was

charming, very intelligent, and well read. And she, probably bored in that solitude, also looked forward to my company. We spent long hours talking about books, art, and the theater. It was a pleasure to remove myself from reality and enter a world of moral and aesthetic values, one that I feared might vanish forever.

Lena's mother and brother lived on an estate nearby. Their housekeeper had just left, and they were looking for a reliable replacement. Did I happen to know of such a person? Lena would appreciate it very much if I could recommend someone. It occurred to me immediately that a remote estate would be an ideal place for Celinka's mother; Mrs. Górska, as she called herself then, was looking for such a job. I got in touch with Celinka, and the interview with Lena's brother was arranged. Mrs. Górska made an excellent impression; both parties were very happy with the arrangement. Lena's mother was a very pleasant person and treated Mrs. Górska with respect and appreciation for the high quality of her work. It seemed that Celinka's mother had found a safe harbor until the end of the war.

But again, as so often in the past, we were too optimistic. The estate was on the edge of one of the many forests in that region. One day, toward evening, a middle-aged Jewish couple emerged from the forest, worn out, in rags, and hungry. Mrs. Górska invited them to the kitchen and gave them the leftovers from her employer's table. After that evening the couple came to Mrs. Górska's kitchen regularly. Lena's mother was aware of their visits, but never spoke a word of disapproval.

But one day the owner of the house, Lena's brother, returned home earlier than usual and caught the Jews taking their meal. In a rage, he locked them in a room and phoned the police. The Polish police had no choice but to notify the German gendarmes. Even if by chance there had been someone at the police station who wanted to save these people, the phone call from the manor could not be disregarded.

In no time, the German gendarmes arrived and took the Jews outside. About fifteen minutes later, Mrs. Górska heard several shots. The next day she learned that the Germans had ordered a peasant in a neighboring cottage to take the corpses away and bury them somewhere.

All that night, Lena's mother knelt by the crucifix and prayed on behalf of her son the murderer. Evidently, mother and son did not speak about what had happened. Of course, Mrs. Górska could not stay in the house any longer. Nobody suspected her of being Jewish, nor was she reprimanded because she had let the Jews into her employer's house. She could not stay because she could not bear to live under the same roof with a murderer. She found some excuse and left. Soon she found another job that offered her a safe place to live.

Mrs. Górska was a very strong woman, and she told me this story in a matter-of-fact manner. But it had not been easy for her to recover from the shock.

I think that Lena knew what had happened in her brother's house and guessed that I also knew. But she never alluded to the murder. Nor did she ask me to help her find another housekeeper for her mother.

Much later I started wondering what kind of person the murderer was. What had brought him to this terrible act? What were the motives for a seemingly intelligent person who was held in esteem in the neighborhood to commit murder? At the time, however, only facts mattered to us. We took an interest in a person's character and intentions only when he or she could spell danger. The moment Mrs. Górska left her employer's house, the case was closed.

But what happened after the war? What did we do about this outrageous crime committed so close to us? We did nothing. I recall that once or twice I talked to Celinka about it. I do not remember her answer, but I seem to remember her gesture—it was like brushing away a nagging fly.

I wondered why Celinka and her mother, both women with the highest moral standards, were in this instance so indifferent. Why did the three of us, so strongly opposed to the delays in punishing the war criminals, do nothing when we could contribute to the cause of justice?

Were we so absorbed with our new life after the war that there was no place in our minds for the recent past? Was it opportunism, fear of getting involved in "Jewish business"? It worries me. Now I realize how often we are ready to blame someone else. When I read the lines I have just written, I feel that I am inclined to blame Celinka more than myself because she was more involved than I in the events. But I know that this is a kind of excuse to clear my conscience. Many times, when I listen to someone's recollections or read memoirs from this time, I have an impression that, consciously or unconsciously, people avoid remembering those details that are embarrassing to themselves.

The New Tenants

AFTER HAVING THE VILLA to ourselves, Danka, Janek, and I were not pleased when the owner installed some paying tenants in two rooms upstairs. They were a young couple, Aleksy and Olga, and Aleksy's mother. That they were of Russian origin was evident from the mother's heavy accent. The young people had probably been born in Poland or had come as children.

We were unhappier still when we learned that mother and son were guards at the Pawiak prison on Pawia Street in Warsaw, notorious for its cruelty since 1863, when political prisoners were first sent there following the January uprising against Russia. It has served as a prison for political offenders ever since. The mother worked in the women's section, known as Serbianka. Under the Nazis, the Pawiak was a place where prisoners were tortured and often killed.

The guards assigned to political prisoners have always been known for their harshness. Many, in fact, were degenerates who chose the work so they could satisfy their sadistic proclivities. Of course, there were exceptions: good people were sometimes mentioned in prisoners' memoirs.

When Janek heard what line of work the tenants were in, he was panic-stricken. At first he thought I should move out. But I had nowhere to go, and Danka strongly objected to my leaving. She convinced Janek that I would know how to handle the situation.

In spite of our fears, the new tenants made a good impression. The mother was energetic and good-natured. Aleksy was very handsome, with his prominent cheek-bones and very blue eyes. He had good manners and was very sociable; in the evenings he treated us generously to vodka. Danka pointed out that his company on the train home from work actually made my trip safer. This "true Slav" in his official uniform was an excellent cover to ward off any attempt at blackmail. She was right, though who could have foreseen that he would lead me to blackmail from a different vantage point?

On our way home across the sands that stretched from the railroad station in Radość to our place in Zbójna Góra, we would pass one of the numerous illegal bakeries in the region, where bread and rolls were baked from grain hidden from the Germans. The peasants were permitted to keep only a small portion of their grain; the rest was to be delivered to the authorities for a ridiculously low fee, part in money and part—to demoralize the populace—in vodka. The Germans managed to increase the consumption of alcohol, but they could not keep the peasants from hiding their grain. Polish peasants knew how to protect themselves from the demands of an occupying power, and they went on baking bread and rolls. In rare periods of "prosperity," when I had some spare groszy, I would buy a very fresh loaf—it resembled French bread—for Danka and me. What a delicacy! No bread ever tasted so good.

Once, when Aleksy and I were passing a bakery located well away from the road, Aleksy said, "Zofia, I have a great idea. These bakers are loaded. If we threaten to denounce them, they would pay whatever we ask."

I saw that he considered this a stroke of genius. I stiffened. I would not have been surprised by an attempt to blackmail me if my charming companion had had the slightest suspicion that I was Jewish. But to be invited to take part in a blackmail scheme? No, this would never, under any circumstances, have crossed my mind. Although I realized immediately that Aleksy's proposition was proof of his confidence in me and his appreciation of my intelligence, I was shocked and terrified. First I had to overcome my revulsion. I could not let him know that I despised him, that he made me sick. Relax, I told myself. Not to be taken by surprise, to be prepared for anything—that was the secret of survival. In such dangerous situations I had learned to remain calm and self-possessed.

"What a great idea, Aleksy!" I replied. "And that money would certainly come in handy."

I stopped talking, as if I were about to set up a specific plan of action in the next sentence. After a long pause, I began to talk slowly, as if thinking aloud. "You know, I am worried about one thing. This could be dangerous for *us*. We are the only strangers here from Warsaw. All these people have known one another for years and almost all of them are involved in the bakeries; one buys grain, another grinds it, somebody else bakes the bread, still others sell the stuff. We would be the first to be suspected of organizing this business." Deliberately, I avoided use of the right word—blackmail. "Some dark night we might be knifed."

I had played my hand well. Aleksy became upset as the prospect of easy money faded. Yet my reasoning was convincing, and the danger I cautioned him against was real. Thus, I proved to be a businesslike young lady—and a smart one as well. Our "friendship" was not imperiled. But Danka, Janek, and I now had even more reason to be wary of the new tenants.

My Charming Cousin

I TRIED TO BE as alert as possible. Yet sometimes I got mixed up in troubles that certainly could have been avoided. One day on the street in Warsaw I met my cousin Paula. I had never liked her—and for good reason. Among my bad memories of her was one particularly disgusting incident during my stay in the ghetto. I had been caught on Ogrodowa Street in one of the frequent roundups and had to find a hiding place right away. I was a few blocks away from my relatives' apartment. They had a shelter in a cellar, and I located its entrance. There were many people there; the air was dense, and a newcomer could have been considered an additional drain on the limited amount of stored food. However, because of the danger, nobody objected to my entering the shelter. Only my cousin Paula made a big fuss, demanding that I clear out. Other relatives, furious with her, told her to shut up. I stayed in the cellar until the danger was over.

When I met her on the Aryan side, I forgot my grudges and was happy that she had escaped from the ghetto. She asked me if I could recommend a trustworthy Pole who would keep some of the belongings she had smuggled out. I directed her to my schoolmate, Cesia Szczypińska.

Later, when I saw Cesia, she was very angry with me: "How could you send such a terrible person to me?" Cesia told me that my cousin had wanted to make friends with her. While pretending to praise me and my ability to "charm" people, she implied that I was insincere and motivated by a personal interest in establishing useful friendships with Poles. She meant that I only pretended to like Cesia because I needed her, that I manipulated her.

Cesia was disgusted. She cut Paula off, saying that she had known me for years and never noticed a trace of insincerity in me. "Even if Zofia were deceitful," she told Paula, "it was mean to try to change my friendly feeling toward her. All you gained was my disgust for you. Find someone else to safeguard your belongings. I don't want to see you again."

After such experiences I should have avoided any contact with Paula. But when I met her again one night shortly before the curfew, she was in despair; she had miraculously escaped from the hands of blackmailers who had robbed her place and intended to hand her over to the Gestapo. She had no place to go.

I could not let Paula spend the night in the streets; that meant certain death. I told her to come with me. I warned her of our tenants, the prison guards: I made it clear that she could only stay overnight, to avoid being seen by them.

There was a family likeness between Paula and me which would increase the possibility of tracing some of our Jewish characteristics. That often happened when more than one Jew was present, particularly when they were relatives.

Danka approved my decision to let Paula stay overnight. When I left Radość early in the morning, Paula was still there, pretending that she wanted to rest a few hours more after her terrifying experiences of the previous day. When I came home that evening and opened the door, I heard Danka yelling, "Get out of here! Right now!"

From Danka's chaotic account I could figure out what had happened. Paula had offered Danka a huge monthly payment in return for shelter in the villa. The only condition was that I move out. She tried to persuade Danka to consider her own situation. She used the same arguments she had tried with Cesia: "Zofia would easily find another place. Zofia knows how to 'get around' people and make friends. Zofia is so smart."

Foolishly, she judged others by her own character; she easily forgot favors she had received as well as pain she had inflicted. Since she had money and I did not, she believed she had the upper hand. She was sure she could buy Danka.

"What a swine!" exclaimed Danka. "She betrayed you. You who rescued her. She tried to bribe me." I had to calm Danka and ask her to let Paula stay one more night. We could not let her go so close to the curfew.

In the morning, Paula left, screaming insults at Danka, but mostly ranting at me for putting a relative out on the street.

The Ring

FORTUNATELY for Danka and me, Aleksy's family found another apartment in Warsaw. We were happy to get rid of tenants who presented a potential danger to us, and they were happy to find a place in the city. We drank a lot of vodka during the farewell. And we sighed with relief when Aleksy returned for their last valise.

After they left, it became pleasant and quiet. Danka suggested that I move downstairs into the living room; she and Janek would use the rooms upstairs. The living room would be more spacious and convenient for me; she had to get up early in the morning, whereas I preferred to read well into the night and get up later. She warned me to close the shutters of the French window before I went to bed. This I forgot to do.

When I moved downstairs, I took my coat to serve as a

bathrobe; I wanted it close to the bed so I could throw it over my shoulders if I chose to go to the garden before taking a shower upstairs. I awoke in the morning and reached for the coat. To my surprise, it was not where it should have been; my first thought was that I had forgotten to bring it downstairs. I looked around and noticed that my dress was also missing, along with my underclothing and shoes. What had happened? I looked at the French window. It was closed, but then I realized how the thieves had entered the room. They had cut out a piece of glass just big enough for a hand to reach in and turn the key. There was nothing to grab but my clothing: that was all the booty to be found. Later I discovered my shoes at the gate. They were so worn that they were not worth stealing.

The word "booty" might appear exaggerated for a few pieces of old clothing, but for me the theft was disastrous. It was not the loss of my coat; fortunately, I had another, left in Mrs. Uklejska's apartment. For a few minutes, I stood naked and distressed in the living room. Then I wrapped myself in a blanket and went upstairs to tell Danka and Janek what had happened. I was so upset that I blurted out that there had been a gold bracelet sewn into the lining of my coat, a present my parents had given me the day I graduated from the university. I had smuggled it out of the ghetto and had left it hidden for a real emergency, though I had always hoped that I would manage to hold on to it for its sentimental value. When I left Lodz, it was the one valuable I was persuaded to take; I thought my parents would need jewelry more than I. It didn't weigh much and had no great monetary worth, but it was a fine piece of old craftsmanship. And what counted most for me—it was the only gift from my parents that I still possessed.

I had never mentioned my bracelet to Danka and Janek. Not that I considered it a secret, but there was no reason to tell them. I should not have mentioned its loss. But I could not foresee their reaction—they were more upset than I was. A gold bracelet! A Jewish gold bracelet! That was certainly a treasure. My friends were very unhappy about my loss and very angry with me. Why had I been so careless? Why had I not paid attention and closed the shutters? They blamed me most for not telling them about the "treasure"; they would certainly have found a safe place for it. I had the impression that the sensational news stirred some strange feelings in them, particularly in Janek. He was doing so much for me, yet was gaining not a penny. Now it was thieves who had profited (provided they discovered the bracelet before they sold the coat in some flea market). And the theft seemed to reinforce a stereotype so often heard among Poles: "No matter what, the Jews have gold." My friends tried to conceal their reaction, but I sensed what they were thinking and found it painful.

I possessed one more valuable. It was a platinum ring with a small diamond, sent to me from Lodz by my beloved Aunt Ida Reznik, my mother's oldest sister. Though the Lodz ghetto was closed, almost hermetically so, there were a few illegal channels of communication created for mutual profit by Germans and certain Jews who collaborated with them. Aunt Ida had used those channels to send me the only valuable thing she possessed. I had given it to Danka for safekeeping.

A couple of days after the theft, Janek took the ring

from Danka's hiding place. He announced that we—meaning Danka and me—were not to be trusted. The theft proved it. He blamed Danka too, even though she had told me to close the shutters. From now on, he would take care of the ring, he said. That would be best for me, he believed. Danka and I were astonished and angry: Janek had not volunteered his services as keeper of the ring; he had just taken it, a fait accompli. Danka was even angrier than I was. Ultimately, though, Janek gave in to Danka's rage and my resentment and returned the ring.

My property was restored, but my feelings were still hurt. Certainly there was some truth in what he had said; he did consider himself a more responsible guardian of the ring than Danka and I were. Yet I suspected that there was something else on his mind. I wondered whether it did not occur to him that if—God forbid—I were caught by the Germans, he would have been my "natural" heir. Would it not have been fair recompense for the risks to which he exposed himself and his girlfriend? This was my conjecture, and maybe there was some injustice in it. Yet events had proved that the Jews could not take for granted the help they received from the Poles. It happened that decent and courageous Poles sometimes could not bear the constant threat we presented. With tears in their eyes, they sometimes begged their Jewish tenants to move out. Even when only one member of the family lost his courage, the others could not resist the pressure.

And it was not uncommon for people who had sheltered Jews disinterestedly or for a decent fee suddenly to begin blackmailing them. It was widely held that anyone who missed the opportunity to profit (and Jews furnished the "golden" opportunity) was a sucker; if a person failed to use his head, it was his tough luck. You could even kick him for it. This attitude showed a dangerous contempt for humane values and even for mere decency. There was acceptance, if not approval, of behavior which a normal, healthy society would have condemned and punished. Under such conditions, even decent people sometimes lapsed and indulged themselves. This occurred with Janek, but it was only a deviation, a temptation he overcame. He remained honest and loyal, and deserves respect for his compassion and courage.

A postscript is necessary, lest I omit a bitter word about myself. The theft of my coat would have been a disaster for me if I hadn't had another coat—the one I wore the first time I left the ghetto with the labor brigade, and then entrusted to Mrs. Uklejska. The last time I left the ghetto, I had worn my other coat, the one that was stolen.

Oddly, the possession of two coats made me uneasy. I felt that I should have given one of them to Celinka, who had a very old, shabby coat that she wore summer and winter. Many times I was about to tell her that I had another coat and that I was going to give it to her. Yet I did not. Was it my vanity—both coats were very becoming to me. Was I too attached to material things? Anyway, I did not do what I ought to have done.

When my coat was stolen, my selfishness was rewarded. I was fortunate to have another coat, but I did not feel lucky at all. Celinka never learned where I found the second coat. Yet a certain dissatisfaction with myself lingers after so many years, whenever my memory brings back to me the providential coat.

The Secret of Stenya and Anya

As soon as the prison guards left the villa in Radość, Janek energetically began to look for other tenants; he was eager to forestall the owner, who could again have imposed undesirable people on us. Janek could not have done better. He found two cousins, Stenya Adamska and Anya Kaminska, and Stenya's boyfriend, Staszek Laskowski. The three certainly did not present any threat to us. The older cousin, Anya, was in her early forties. (That is what I believed then—and what she wanted to be believed. Not until she died, in 1976, did I learn that she was ten years older.) She had gleaming silver hair, and her beautiful eyes, almost violet, were full of tenderness and wisdom. She had a lovely pale pink complexion and her smile revealed dimples in her cheeks. Her most telling trait was her bearing; she had the natural elegance of a great lady.

The younger cousin, Stenya, was about my age and was one of the most attractive girls I have ever met. Her dark, curly hair was cut short, and her dark blue eyes were a little slanted. Like her older cousin, she had charming dimples in her cheeks. She was taller than the average man, and she stooped a little, as if she wanted to seem shorter. What a cheerful, intelligent, friendly girl she was.

Staszek, Janek's colleague at the office and a member of the underground army, had a pleasant, youthful air and a fair, open face which at once invited confidence. His appearance was marred only by two missing front teeth, probably lost in one of the fights he would get into after drinking too much vodka. Staszek adored Stenya, but she, usually so easygoing and friendly, was often sharp with him, even when he didn't seem to deserve it. Stenya explained to me that she couldn't stand his drinking. It was not for me to say what the trouble really was, but I guessed it had something to do with the difference in their upbringing and background.

The two cousins worked in an office, probably for low salaries, but their standard of living was incomparably higher than Danka's and mine. At that time the standard was measured chiefly by the quantity and quality of the food people consumed.

I was often invited to the cousins' apartment for supper. Anya, the head of their modest household, was the cook. Her specialty was potato pancakes. Anya's pancakes were delicious. After the war I used to ask Anya to make them for me. They were always very good, but they never tasted as great as the ones she treated me to in Radość. We also drank quite a lot of vodka, but nobody could match Staszek. Maybe he drank so much because of the danger he was exposed to in the underground. Or maybe he drank because of his unrequited love for Stenya.

Stenya and I became as close as we would have been had we known each other all our lives. Anya treated me with the motherly tenderness I needed so much; the last time I had seen my own mother was in 1939. In spite of our mutual trust, I did not tell them I was Jewish. I did not want to involve them in my affairs: they probably had enough problems of their own. I also wanted to stick to my plan of adapting to my surroundings, and to maintain as long as I could the role I had been playing.

Shortly after the new tenants moved in, a friend of theirs called on them in Radość. He was introduced to me by his first name, Zbig. He was unusually handsome, with dark hair, intelligent brown eyes, and charming manners. When Stenya and Anya left for work, he stayed with me, and I enjoyed the company of this bright and very well-read young man. I can't remember how it happened that we began to talk about Marcel Proust's *Remembrance of Things Past*, about Swann's desire to enter high society and the appearance he conveyed of somehow not being himself—or of being many selves. Zbig, in an odd way, reminded me of Swann. I was almost certain that he was a Jew whom the cousins were helping. Everyone had a secret during the war, and sooner or later some of the secrets were disclosed.

And so it was with Stenya's and Anya's secrets. It was Celinka who let the secret out. When she came to visit me in Radość, I was happy to tell her that the prison guards had left and that wonderful new tenants had replaced them. At that moment Stenya and Anya were in the garden; both liked gardening very much. Celinka took a look at them through the window and began to laugh. "Don't you know who they are? That's Zula Sterling and her mother, Ludwika."

Anya—Ludwika Sterling—was the widow of a lawyer well known for his defense of political prisoners. The Sterlings were an old, distinguished Jewish family, assimilated for more than a century and remembered for their contribution to the Polish uprising against tsarist rule in 1863–64. There is still in Lodz a Dr. Sterling Street, named in honor of Zula's uncle, a noted physician and philanthropist.

Anya was twenty years younger than her husband. She could have remarried after he died, but she did not. Instead, she devoted herself entirely to her children.

Celinka also let out the secret of Zbig, in whom I had already recognized a Jew. He was Stenya's—Zula's—former husband, whom she had divorced before she met Staszek. This brilliant, rather neurotic man seemed better suited to Zula than Staszek, though, as Zula admitted later, he was not easy to live with. Undoubtedly, Staszek was more open and generous, but she soon broke off with him. He became Celinka's boyfriend for a short time. I heard later that his body was found somewhere in the countryside: he had been killed and robbed of his shoes, probably in a drunkards' fight.

I refer to Stenya now by her true name, Zula, the name she returned to after the war. Everybody called her by it, and I think of her thus. Her mother, though, I refer to as Anya, the name she assumed during the war. She probably preferred it, and it is how she remains in my memory.

I assumed that their Jewish origins did not give the "cousins" too much trouble, and that they had given their considerable resources for safekeeping to their numerous Polish friends or to the Catholic members of their family.

Later, however, Zula told me that they had had a very hard time. After the war broke out, Zula and Zbig fled to Lvov, where he could finish his medical studies. When the Soviets began to deport the refugees from Poland to remote regions of Russia, the couple decided to return to Warsaw. Anya sent them a guide from Warsaw, whom she paid in advance to facilitate their trip. The guide appeared in their apartment in Lvov and demanded money. Since they had none, they gave him Zula's engagement ring. He did not show up for their appointment at the railroad station. What for? The Jews had already paid him twice.

Anya had also had her share of disappointments. Her numerous Polish friends—all but two of them—refused to help. She finally moved into the apartment of a schoolmate, Mrs. Kłys, whose husband was in hiding. He was of German extraction but refused German citizenship; this was considered a crime. The one time Mrs. Kłys had to delay payment to the peasant who was hiding her husband, the peasant murdered him.

It was around Christmastime when Zula appeared in Mrs. Kłys's apartment. Hungry and sick, she was suffering from an acute rash, probably due to malnutrition. When her hostess was out, Zula used to take some pork grease on her fingertips and spread it over the most painful areas of her skin. Once she found an old tube of facial cream. She was about to throw it away but gave it a last squeeze. There was no cream, but she felt a small hard object. When she cut the tube with scissors, she found a gold rouble, known as a "piggy." It probably had been hidden there during one of Mrs. Kłys's prewar trips abroad, since taking gold or any hard currency out of the country was strictly regulated. Later, it had been forgotten. It was a small coin of no great value, but for Zula it was a treasure. Her mother wanted her to return it to Mrs. Kłys immediately, but Zula took a firm stand against this. Mrs. Kłys, she argued, had forgotten the coin and was relatively well off, whereas she, Zula, was very hungry. She took the rouble to a friend who knew some dealers in hard currency. She sold it and bought a lot of food.

Soon Anya and Zula had to move out. The police frequently invaded Mrs. Kłys's apartment, looking for her husband. Anya found a position as a maid in a rich friend's house. She used to say that no outfit ever suited her better than the little white apron and white bonnet the maids were expected to wear in fashionable houses.

One day a friend of her employer came to visit. Anya, in her maid's uniform, brought tea and cookies on a silver tray. The man, a literary critic, cast a glance at her, smiled, and said to the hostess: "I see you are employing a Miss Rothschild."

Whatever she wore and whatever she did, Anya always looked dignified, and her manner might well have suggested a once-high social standing. And because it was impossible to predict whether the guest would make any use of his discovery of "Miss Rothschild" in maid's disguise, Anya packed her bag and left, so as not to endanger her employer. She spent the night at a railroad station, an especially dangerous place for a Jew, since blackmailers and gendarmes often searched there for people on the wanted list. It was a great relief when her friend and former landlady, Mrs. Kłys, offered to rent her a small apartment, a room and kitchen, in a house on Wielka Street. Now mother and daughter had a place to themselves—an ideal solution, or so it seemed.

But of course there were no ideal solutions. In a few days, they met a man—a tenant in their building—who had worked for the electric company and had known them before the war. He had also made some small repairs in their house and had been well paid for them. He pretended not to recognize the women; he did not even raise his hat. Under the circumstances, such discretion was desirable. But who knew what to make of it? Would he be tempted, like so many others, to put his finger in the Jewish pie? Would he send an accomplice, since he himself was known to the ladies?

In fact, blackmailers soon appeared in their new apartment, and the women had to look for other shelter. Fortunately, they met Staszek Laskowski. He lived across the courtyard and had an excellent observation post when Zula washed herself in a kitchen basin—often forgetting to pull down the shade. When Staszek began to follow her to the office and back home, the women thought that another blackmailer had appeared on the scene. For once, this was not the case. Staszek, enchanted by Zula's beauty, had fallen in love with her. Thus their romance started. But romance is perhaps the wrong word for their relationship. They were a mismatched couple. Zula accepted Staszek's love but did not reciprocate it. Was it too painful to reject his affection? Or was such devotion too desirable to be rejected under the circumstances? It is not for me to say; probably all these feelings were involved.

When the opportunity arose to rent two rooms in the villa in Radość, Zula and Anya happily left their place on Wielka Street. Danka, Janek, and I welcomed them warmly, and we were to remain lifelong friends.

The End of the Romance

ONE EVENING, after our correspondence with Bednarek had gone on for some time and my fears that this could disrupt her life had subsided, Danka presented me with a new idea. "You know, I can take a few days off and go to Lvov to meet Bednarek. Just for fun. Don't I deserve some fun?" And to forestall my objections and put me off guard she added, "It will do me good. This is the only way to get him out of my head once and for all." She was fully aware, she said, that Bednarek had stolen the best of her young years, that he had deceived her, and she knew her future was with Janek. She invoked heaven as her witness that there would be no affair with Bednarek; she wasn't that stupid. She rehearsed her meeting with him as if it were taking place on a stage: she would act like a lady.

"You should trust me. You know I would never deceive

Janek. This will be my revenge on Bednarek for all he has done to me." Nothing I said made a bit of difference. She had already made up her mind. There was nothing to do but help her refurbish her much-worn dresses, and with a heavy heart tell her, "Have a good time."

A few weeks passed. When she returned, Danka was very quiet about her vacation, not her usual self. I guessed that things hadn't gone according to her script. Soon I learned what had happened: Danka was pregnant. She had no doubt that Bednarek was the father; she had carefully avoided any sexual contact with Janek since her return from Lvov. I had the impression that her feelings for him had cooled after she'd renewed her romance with Bednarek. She was honest and didn't want to deceive Janek; she wanted to be absolutely sure who the father was. And she probably believed that Bednarek under these circumstances would come back to her for good.

We had long, feverish discussions about what to do. Certainly I was more of an opportunist—or maybe less honest—than Danka; I advised her to conceal the truth from Janek. I thought I could find a gynecologist for an abortion; Janek need never learn what had happened. Danka wouldn't listen. Most people didn't want children in wartime, and living with me, Danka was particularly exposed to danger. If something happened to me, she could have been arrested and the child abandoned. But she wanted this child.

To make her decision irrevocable, she proposed that I accompany her when she went to pray for the child, as if to commit herself before God. Since she knew I would refuse to go to church, she found an alternative she knew I couldn't reject—the cemetery at Powązki where Kazia, her stepsister, who had died of consumption, was buried. We would pray at Kazia's grave and Kazia, in heaven, would intercede for us.

It was a beautiful day, typical of a Polish autumn: the ground was covered with leaves that were still golden-brown. They crackled under our feet as we walked slowly, not talking, each of us deep in her own thoughts. From time to time we stopped to look at a gravestone or read an inscription. The silence was perfect and I felt a peacefulness I had not known for a very long time. Perhaps I felt safe and reconciled to life when I was among the dead.

All of a sudden Danka stopped walking and cried out, "Look at this!" Her finger pointed to the tiny grave of a child. It was clear that no one had visited it for a long time; it was overgrown with weeds. But the inscription was clear. It read:

Here lies Zofia Sielczak of blessed memory, our angel who has gone to heaven. May she look down on us and help us in our need.

It was followed by the date of birth of the child and the names of her parents.

There was no doubt about it. The date and names corresponded exactly to those on the birth certificate copied for me at the Church of Saint John on Sowia Street. The real Zofia Sielczak had found her resting place here. And here was I—Zofia Rubinstein—who had been denied the right to live and in spite of that continued to live under the name of the long-dead child.

I was excited by this discovery. And suddenly I began to laugh. Danka laughed, too. Indeed, there was no reason to mourn little Zofia, who was unknown to us. Danka considered the coincidence a good omen. I don't remember which of us had the idea, but we went back to the cemetery gates and bought two small bunches of flowers from an old woman who also sold candles and devotional articles. One bunch we put on Zofia Sielczak's little grave, the other on the grave of Danka's stepsister. Danka knelt there and prayed for Kazia and for her own unborn child. "I prayed also for your happy survival of the war," she told me. I was moved beyond speech.

The time had come to notify Bednarek that he was going to be a father. My heart was heavy as I sat down to write the letter, which turned out to be our last to him. We didn't have to wait long for the answer. I was stunned. The wording of his cruel and vulgar letter was unforgettable. He called Danka names: she was a cow that opened her legs to every bull. He wanted nothing to do with this bastard of hers. He cared nothing for her. He would answer no more letters.

After all these years I still feel embarrassed when I recall those words. I felt for Danka; I imagined she was in despair. But she was strangely calm, and made no comment. I began to hope that she might change her mind about having the baby, since all chances of reviving the affair with Bednarek were gone. But she did not reconsider her decision. In spite of what she had suffered at Bednarek's hands, she still wanted his child—something nobody, not even he, could take away from her. Her determination was terribly touching.

We heard no more from Bednarek. If Danka heard anything about him, she didn't tell me. After the war, she made inquiries—she told me this years later—but there was not a trace of him. Perhaps he had escaped to the West. Or maybe he was killed when the Russian Army entered Lvov.

I tried to persuade Danka not to tell Janek the truth about her pregnancy, to tell him that he was the father. This would be less painful for everybody and best for the baby. But Danka wouldn't follow my advice. Perhaps she was more honest than I, or still nursed illusions that Bednarek would change his mind. Of course, telling Janek the truth meant the end of their love story as well.

King Tut's Leg

LIFE DID NOT SPARE ME annoying difficulties—but they were bearable as long as they did not affect the main Jewish problem: to survive. In normal circumstances, a fractured foot could be considered no more than a misadventure. Yet, on the Aryan side, it had serious consequences. Early one afternoon Danka and I went to Warsaw. The train was so crowded that when passengers pushed toward the exit, one scarcely moved under one's own power but was swept along by the human tide. Between the train and the platform was a gap about fifteen inches wide; as I tried to step across it, I received a strong push from behind and my left foot got caught. I screamed, but it took awhile for people to stop pushing so that I could extricate it.

The pain was excruciating. I felt I was going to faint. My

foot was obviously broken and needed immediate attention. Hopping on my good leg and leaning on Danka's shoulder, I left the railroad station. The nearest first-aid post was a twenty-minute walk; I could not make it. Danka tried to bargain with a driver of a *riksha*, a bicycle to which a cart for passengers was attached, but the driver wanted twelve zlotys and we didn't even have that amount. At this critical moment a good angel appeared dressed in the uniform of a motorman. He offered to pick me up in his arms and carry me to a doctor. "It is so easy," he said. "The young lady is so light."

Jaś Grabowski, who so gallantly introduced himself to us, was a pleasant-looking black-haired man with friendly brown eyes. He was well known among his colleagues, as I later learned, for his love of adventure and his readiness to help others. It was said that he even drove his streetcar with panache. He held me with great care, protecting my broken foot.

At the first-aid post they put an elastic bandage on my foot. Since I needed a cast, I had to see a doctor in the emergency room of a hospital. Again Jaś carried me, this time to the hospital at the corner of Aleje Niepodległości and Hoża Street. Then he said goodbye to us, giving me a piece of paper with his address on it, "in case you young ladies need me." Danka also gave him our address in Radość.

My difficulties, however, were not over. The nurse in the emergency room asked us to pay in advance. I had no money and was in great pain. I needed the cast right away so that I could get on the train before the curfew. I shouted that I was not going to leave the hospital without seeing the doctor. The nurse shouted they would not let me in until I paid. I raised hell, until the doctor dashed out of the operating room, also shouting.

My instinct told me that this doctor with his funny fuzzy crop of hair was a good person. I told him what had happened, and he put a cast on my leg up to my knee and told me to come to his house the next time I needed help. I began to believe that I had been born under a lucky star. Whenever I got in trouble, someone came to my rescue. I confided in Dr. Trojanowski that I was Jewish.

"I knew it at once," he said. "No money, no place to stay the night, a desperate situation. I would have been surprised if you were not Jewish."

Later we came to know each other and he often aided my Jewish friends. Thanks to him, Celinka could earn some money as well; he recommended her to his patients as a nurse. Though overworked and tired, he was good company, optimistic, and always ready to lend a hand. "Taking care of your leg was worth doing: it saved you your head," he told me when we met after the war.

With the heavy cast on my leg, and a cast shoe, I could move, but dragging the leg along the sidewalk was difficult. With wry sentimentality I christened it Tutankhamen because it looked like the wrappings of a mummy. The cast, moreover, was not without its advantages. Since people generally noticed what seemed unusual, I believed they would be more interested in my leg than in my face. I would be safe from blackmailers, at least for the time being. Again, I was wrong.

One sunny Sunday afternoon, a stranger knocked at the door of the villa in Radość. He asked to see me. Danka had forebodings, but she ushered him into the room where I was lying on my bed reading a book. The stranger entered the room and asked to speak to me in private. "Since the gentleman has a private matter to discuss," I said to Danka, "leave us alone for a few minutes."

I pretended to think that the matter concerned him and not me and that I was being discreet, though I was fully aware that it was me he had in mind, and I knew exactly why. I apologized for being in bed and explained that my foot was broken. "What can I do for you?" I asked politely.

Just as politely he explained that he was a detective in the Kriminal Polizei (the German-controlled police agency that was assigned to investigate common crimes, but was also engaged in searching out Jews). His office had received a report that a Jewess using the name Sielczak was hiding here. Would I please show him my Kennkarte?

I knew that I was in big trouble. My Kennkarte would do me no good, since the authorities knew about the two Zofia Sielczaks, both of whose IDs were based on the birth certificate of a child long dead.

If I could gain time—that was my first thought. The second was, How could gaining time help me? How could I deal with a Kriminal Polizei officer? Was he really an official or an ordinary blackmailer pretending to be one? Had a report indeed been received by the Kriminal Polizei? Was he acting in an official capacity or on his own?

To gain time . . . !

"I will show you my Kennkarte. But first—with whom am I speaking, please?"

My visitor took an ID out of his wallet, and I could see the official name and stamp of the Kriminal Polizei. I took it from his hand and read it. What could I gain by this?

Yet something caught my attention. The name on the ID was Rososzczuk. Where had I heard that name before?

It was a rather uncommon name, but it sounded familiar to me. My memory—always ready to store information and furnish me with details at the right moment—came to the rescue. I knew this fellow, and it made all the difference.

As I have said, anyone who changed his address was obliged to register with the vital-records office or with the police. Danka hadn't wanted me to register in Radość, where people might be inquisitive about a newcomer, as often happens in villages. She thought I should register as a resident of the building in the city where her stepbrother, Mietek, lived. But she quickly gave up this idea because one of the tenants there was with the Kriminal Polizei and could cause trouble. She had told me all this in great detail, including the name of the detective: Rososzczuk. My memory brought this detail to the surface just at the right moment.

Now, I knew that Rososzczuk's story about information against me having been received by his office was invented so he could blackmail me. It was bad news for me that he really was a detective. But my knowing that he was acting on his own, as of course he was not permitted to do, spoiled his prospects. Perhaps he was also afraid of having other tenants hear about his attempt to blackmail me.

I still had Rososzczuk's ID in my hand. To his surprise, I got up slowly from my bed and, limping—more than usual—I went to the door, opened it, and called Danka. "Come upstairs! Do you know who our guest is? This is Mr. Rososzczuk, Mietek's neighbor."

Danka at once caught the import of this news and knew how to play the game. In a minute she was in my room. "What a surprise! Such a guest! Welcome, Mr. Rososzczuk!" Then she added, with apparent embarrassment, "What can I treat you to? All we have in the house is a mug of buttermilk."

Not waiting for our guest's answer, she brought the buttermilk. Her hospitality had a clear purpose: he should know that we were poor as could be. In fact, there *was* nothing to eat or drink in the house but the buttermilk, and this added conviction to Danka's excellent performance. The scoundrel was disconcerted.

Awkwardly, he excused himself for the intrusion: "You know, we receive so many false reports. Who could have known? What terrible times we are living in!"

Danka expressed full understanding, as well as regret that Mr. Rososzczuk had been bothered with misleading information and had had to make an unnecessary trip to Radość. (Incidentally, it was not the first time he had made this trip. The neighbors from the building across the street told us later that several times someone had knocked on our gate.)

Mr. Rososzczuk drank the buttermilk; I sincerely wished he would choke on it. Danka accompanied him to the gate, and I, still playing the invalid, stayed in bed. She told him that she had known me since I was a little girl. She knew my family very well. How could it have happened that his office had received false information about me?

"It could only come from some girl who is jealous of Zofia," she told our visitor. "You know, Zofia is a breaker of men's hearts." The blackmailer could only agree, and left.

In fact, all this was Danka's fault. It was obvious that she had been the source of the information. She admitted that she had told my secret to Bożena, a friend of hers who also lived in her stepbrother's building. Danka was so happy and proud of our friendship that she could not refrain from telling Bożena about me—how good, how intelligent, how well educated I was. Clearly, Bożena had become jealous. She had probably grown up in the same world as Danka, where accounts were squared with a knife or a denunciation. By denouncing me to Rososzczuk, she was avenging herself on Danka for what she considered the betrayal of their friendship. Danka bitterly deplored her own stupidity.

There was no immediate danger. But Rososzczuk certainly knew that the report he had received from Bożena was true despite Danka's swearing by all that's holy that I was Catholic. He also must have had a good look at me during our conversation. It was possible that he already had an accomplice or would find one and would try again. So I was out of danger only for a short time.

The first thing I thought it necessary to do was to tell Anya and Zula the story. I did not let on that I knew their true identity; I only explained that it was my duty to tell them about a blackmailer who might return; perhaps they had reason to avoid contact with someone in the Kriminal Polizei. Anya appreciated my thoughtfulness. In accordance with the rules of the game, she still—even at this juncture—kept their identity a secret. Although it made sense for them to leave, she said, they had no place else to go; they would take the risk and stay.

But I could not take the risk. It was very hard for me to leave Danka, and even harder for her. She racked her brain for a way to avoid the separation, and the evening after Rososzczuk's visit, she approached me with an extraordinary idea.

"You buy another Kennkarte and make it out in your name, Zofia, with my family name. You will be my sister. If anything happened to you, even if you were caught by the Gestapo"—she crossed herself—"I would go and swear that we were sisters, with the same mother and father. I would snatch you out of their clutches."

What a magnanimous, incredibly courageous offer! I wept, I embraced her, but I could not accept. If I were caught, Danka's oath would not help me. And there would be one more victim—Danka herself. She cried, too, when I explained this to her, but she understood that I had to leave.

The next day I went to Warsaw and told my story to Celinka and Marysia. Again we reviewed our "emergency list" of people who might give me shelter. My friends were very upset about my having to move. And they were surprised when I told them I thought I already had a solution. With complete assurance I told them that there were two people who would offer me a place. One was Jaś Grabowski, the motorman who had carried me to the hospital after my accident; the other was a young man named Tadeusz. (At that time I did not even know his surname.) Tadeusz had been a student at a polytechnical institute, and I had met him a few times when I made phone calls from the stationery store owned by his father around the corner from Miss Okonska's.

Celinka and Marysia were more than skeptical. How could I be so sure that I would be helped by total strangers? What was my certainty based on? I was not endowed with any particular beauty. I was not one of those girls who cast a spell over men. Both men had been very nice to me, but they showed no special fascination. Jaś Grabowski had taken me to the hospital, a rather natural thing to do under the circumstances. Tadeusz had just chatted with me a few times. Yet I knew they would help me. Celinka and Marysia attributed my faith to my enviable powers of the imagination—or to total despair. Yet my luck held, because there were many decent people. Or perhaps it was because I strongly believed that there were many decent people that the people I met responded to my faith in them.

My first choice was Jaś Grabowski. He had already displayed some interest in my health. A few days after the accident, I received a postcard from him asking about my "dear foot." The spelling was incredible: two errors in one five-letter word—*nóżka* (leg) was spelled *nuszka*. Now I answered his card, saying that I wanted to see him. We met and went to a cheap bar. He ordered vodka, quite a lot of it, and some kielbasa and cucumbers.

I described the state of my health with a touch of the dramatic. I told Jaś that the doctor had recommended massages and special exercises for my foot. Otherwise, it might not regain its strength and I would limp for a very long time. But, unfortunately, I could not undergo this treatment; I could not walk from my house to the railroad station in Radość. The problem, I said, was that I had no place to stay in Warsaw.

I didn't even need to ask Jaś to help me. "This is a very small problem," he said. "In fact, no problem at all. I have a very nice apartment on Słowacki Street. You can move in whenever you want."

So the scene unfolded according to my script. I sighed in relief—though too soon, as it happened. Jaś went on talking, clearly excited by the opportunity to help someone, particularly someone in real need. He described his place: he had a big room and a kitchen, overlooking a nice courtyard with fruit trees.

I was silent for a moment, as if considering whether a modest, well-bred girl could move into a bachelor's apartment. Jaś understood what was bothering me and hastened to allay my doubts. "Don't worry," he assured me. "You will sleep in the room and I will sleep in the kitchen. I will not come to you unless you call me."

The effect of this statement was not what he had intended. I think his intentions were pure: he really did want to help me. Yet his promise that he would not come to my room unless I called him clearly indicated that he considered it possible that I would do so. My life was complicated enough. I also noticed that the vodka was going to his head. This alone would make it risky for me to stay in the same apartment with him. I drank as much as he did, but I managed to stay sober. Incidentally, he didn't have enough money to pay the bill, but fortunately, I could help him out with the few zlotys in my purse.

I thanked Jaś very much for his generous offer. I could not make up my mind right then, I said; his offer was so unexpected. He would hear from me soon. We parted true friends or would-be lovers. Of course, I never wrote to him; I never saw him again. But I have preserved a warm remembrance of this gallant and good-natured motorman from Warsaw.

The Little House in Koło

Since I had rejected the good services of Jaś, I had to try my second plan. The next day I was in front of the stationery store on Wilcza Street, and through the store window I saw that I had come at a good time; this was the day Tadeusz worked there. I waited until a customer paid and left, and then I limped—again a little more than was necessary—into the store and asked permission to use the telephone. I dialed a fictitious number and began to talk to a nonexistent friend. I complained that I could not take the treatment the doctor had prescribed. I could not come every day from Radość to Warsaw—it was too much for me. It was clear to anyone who overheard this "conversation" that the response was negative, that my "friend" didn't know about anyone with a room to rent. I voiced my disappointment, said thank you, and hung up. Then I approached the counter to pay for the call.

Everything went as I had planned. Tadeusz apologized for listening to my conversation. If I didn't mind, he said, he would like to help me. By chance, his godmother wanted to rent out a room in her house. She was a widow who lived with her sister; they were both charming ladies. They were looking for an intelligent, trustworthy tenant.

"I could take you to them. Only you'd better say that we were fellow students who have known each other a long time." I agreed with enthusiasm. I would come back in two hours when Tadeusz's father relieved him in the store.

The house was located in Koło, on the outskirts of Warsaw. The suburb had a new section with large apartment houses and an old section, called Wooden Koło, with one- and two-family houses built for city and state employees. Mrs. Kałużniacka, who before the war had been employed in a state savings bank, owned a one-family house on Dobrogniewa Street. The little houses were on one side of the street; on the other side was a stand of trees. The place looked more like a village than a suburb; the house itself was bordered with wild roses. On both sides of the gate stood two evergreens, like sentries watching over the peace of the inhabitants.

Tadeusz introduced me to his godmother, Maria Kałużniacka, and her sister, Janina Ostrowska. He made it clear to the ladies that I had very limited means, so they asked a very modest rent. The room was full of light; a window overlooked a small well-kept garden. The furniture was inexpensive but in good taste. And it was spotless.

"This was my late husband's room," said Mrs. Kałużniacka. "He liked it very much. I hope you will feel comfortable here."

I moved in the next day. On the table in my room, I found a big vase filled with sunflowers. Soon I became very good friends with both ladies. Mrs. Kałużniacka was in her early fifties, though she looked older. She usually wore a garden apron over an old but impeccably clean dress: she was the gardener. She wore a cap on her cropped gray hair to protect her from the sun. Her pale blue eyes were calm and friendly, and her face, which might at first seem common, showed frankness, wisdom, and dignity.

Miss Janina, the younger sister, was very forgetful; when she misplaced things, she lost her temper. She would often get really angry with herself, but sometimes her sister and I became the targets of her bad humor. Mrs. Kałużniacka asked me to pay no attention to these tantrums because Miss Janina was basically good, only unhappy. She had never married, never lived her own life. She had always been in charge of her sister's small household. She was very hard of hearing and that made her even more irritable.

When I came home at night, I found my room cleaned, flowers from the garden on the table, my dress ironed. Miss Janina mended any of my clothes that needed repair. We used to eat together in the kitchen. For breakfast, there was usually soup with potato dumplings, which for some unknown reason Miss Janina called "dumplings with mustaches." For flavor, an ounce of bacon was added. For supper we had vegetables from the garden—potatoes, cucumbers, carrots, cabbage. Mrs. Kałużniacka was an excellent gardener; she made the most of her small plot. The food was often burned or too salty, but I always praised it, not only because I was hungry, but also to please Miss

Janina. "What a good kid Zofia is," she would say. "She likes whatever I cook."

An additional attraction of my new place was the attic library of Mrs. Kałużniacka's late husband. He was an admirer of Balzac, as I was. One could find almost all his novels, as well as books about him. I enjoyed reading these novels, including some I had read before, and Mrs. Kałużniacka was happy that the library was being used again.

Needless to say, I did not go for any medical treatment. That had been just a pretext for finding a place to live. However, every night I soaked my foot in a pail of warm salted water, and in a short time I stopped limping. My accident had helped me to find a safe and pleasant shelter.

After the Germans had entered Warsaw, they closed all Polish banks and Mrs. Kałużniacka had lost her job. Under the occupation, people had to look for new ways to earn a living. The two ladies began to "manufacture" cigarettes; that is, they filled paper cigarette shells with tobacco. They sold them for very little, much less than the Germans charged for the cigarettes produced in the factories under their control. Since both ladies were very busy, I offered to bring home the paper cigarette shells, which were made in illegal workshops in the city.

My landladies had no telephone and they worried about me all day. They knew that I worked in the underground educational network. In any case, everyone was exposed to the German roundups in the streets. When I got home shortly before the curfew, I would often find them waiting impatiently for me at the gates. It was good to know that someone cared. Supper was always ready. I remember I used to say that after the war I would bake a cake as big as the tabletop, with lots of raisins, and I would eat the whole cake in one sitting. Such were our dreams at that time. Since the supper was never enough to satisfy my appetite, I was encouraged by the women to smoke the cigarettes they made. That's how I started smoking; I have been addicted to it ever since.

Soon Miss Janina reminded me that I should register my new address. I did not want to arouse suspicion or make problems for Miss Janina, who was supposed to mail the registration to the vital-records office. So I filled out the form and she mailed it. Yet it was essential that this office should not know my new address; they had been notified of the existence of two Zofia Sielczaks and would have to contact the police if the address of either turned up in their files. So I had to make sure that my registration disappeared as soon as it reached the office.

I knew that Celinka's friend Alek was in the business of forging papers and had the necessary connections in the vital-records office. He promised to see to it that the notice of my new address was removed from the files. Celinka, who had some doubts about Alek's reliability, decided to check up on him. We went together to the vital-records office; I waited outside. She entered the office, pretending that she was looking for the address of her friend, a Zofia Sielczak. To get this information she had to fill out a form with the name and age of the person she was looking for. The clerk looked at the form and then took down a directory marked "S." He looked at the right page, then cast a glance at Celinka and asked her to wait for a moment. He reached for the telephone. Celinka understood immediately that he had seen a notice there that Miss Sielczak was wanted by the police. She did not hesitate. She ran downstairs and took my hand; we turned down the nearest side street to escape any potential danger. Our purpose was served—now we knew that Alek had done his job and that my current address had been taken out of the files. I could safely stay in Mrs. Kałużniacka's house.

Helena's Story, Anda's Poetry

AFTER SEVERAL WEEKS, my stay at Dobrogniewa Street became even more attractive. Since my landladies were happy with me, they decided to look for another tenant. As soon as I met Helena Brodowska, I knew that Providence could not provide better for my landladies or for me. We became lifelong friends.

Helena, like me, was in her twenties. She was short and stocky, with legs somewhat bowed by the rickets that affected children in poor families. But her rosy face was very pretty; she had the blue eyes, ash-blond hair, and high cheekbones characteristic of Polish peasants. Despite her youth, her forehead was furrowed by thought lines; her most striking feature was her friendly grin. One knew immediately that she could be trusted. I told her everything about myself, so there would be at least one person in our small household I did not have to lie to.

In the period between the world wars, educational opportunities were very limited for young people from poor peasant families. But Helena was gifted and strongly motivated to study history. With determination and hard work, she had overcome many obstacles. From her small village in the Lublin region she had come to Warsaw, where she was fortunate enough to meet Professor Helena Radlinska, a prominent progressive educator at the Polish Free University. Helena enrolled in the underground courses set up by this organization during the occupation, concentrating on the history of the Polish peasantry. She used to get up at five o'clock to study. Early one morning she knocked at the door of my room, excited about a provision in Tadeusz Kosciuszko's last will and testament. The hero of the struggle for freedom in Poland and America had left money in his will for the emancipation and education of black slaves, whom he called his "black brothers." I, too, was very much moved; Kosciuszko's words raised my spirits during this time of racism and genocide. So it seemed natural that Helena would wake me at dawn to show me this exciting document.

Helena was a captain in the Peasant Battalions (Bataliony Chłopskie), the military arm of the Peasant Party (Stronnictwo Ludowe). Her activities included helping her Jewish professors and fellow students. One of these Jews suffered from a serious heart ailment and could not walk. Whenever she was compelled to change her hiding place—and this occurred often—Helena had to carry her on her back. With a touch of humor, she said that it was an easy job because her friend, who rarely had enough to eat, weighed very little. (Twenty-four years later, in the Polish People's Republic, she was to defend her fellow teachers when they lost their jobs in the outrageous anti-Semitic campaign of 1967–70.)

In Koło, relations among neighbors were very close. Nobody worried about the curfew; neither the Germans nor the Polish police would risk showing up on Dobrogniewa Street at night. They would have been an easy target for the Polish partisans hiding behind the trees that bordered the street. So social life flourished and there was a lot of visiting back and forth. The neighbors, who liked and respected Mrs. Kałużniacka, took a liking to Helena and me as well, and dropped in on us often.

One evening early in 1944, the talk turned to the price of meat. Miss Janina remarked offhandedly that the demand had been greater in '43 because meat had been smuggled into the ghetto and so was more expensive: "Now it is cheaper, isn't it?" I could not refrain from saying, "I suppose, Miss Janina, that it was worth the murder of half a million people to have the price of meat lowered by twenty groszy."

There was a deep silence in the room. I saw the blood rush to Miss Janina's face. She began stammering; she had never thought—she was just thinking of prices, but it sounded terrible, what she said. It was really a sort of slip of the tongue, because in fact she had deep compassion for the Jews. When the ghetto still existed, she would give food to the Jewish children who sneaked out to get something to eat for themselves and their families. So my outburst was not warranted. However, I was very sensitive to any remark that smelled of anti-Semitism. Helena told me later that I should have had more self-control, that I had been unkind to Miss Janina, a totally innocent person.

On the whole, I felt very safe with my landladies, but I was nevertheless anxious not to betray my Jewishness. I no longer had to pretend that I was a rural teacher, and I could openly acknowledge my university education. But I still had to be careful lest I arouse suspicion; I had to have a family and still keep "alive" my aunt in Zielonka. Once I had a small party at home and invited Cesia and Mrs. Uklejska's daughters Maria and Barbara. I also used to bring home gifts from "family" and friends who, I said, could not visit me. Later, all those "gifts" I returned to their owners—Marysia and Celinka.

I also tried to find some protection in the streetcar when I returned from work; usually it was close to the curfew and often I met the same passengers there. I made friends with some of them, and when I boarded the streetcar, they waved to me cheerfully. This was good cover—I was one of the crowd. A slim, fair-haired youth who usually returned by the same streetcar took a strong liking to me. He would get off with me, although his stop was several blocks farther, and accompany me to the gates of my house. His surname was Żółtko, which means yolk in Polish; oddly enough, he resembled an egg yolk with his yellowish hair and oval face. He was really a bore, but he was very nice to me and an excellent escort on my way home. I valued his company for the safety it provided, but I felt sorry for him in his hopeless courtship.

Fortunately, nobody tried to blackmail me while I was living on Dobrogniewa Street. One day, though, I received

a very unpleasant anonymous letter written in rhyme. It
read:

You use various disguises,
You strut in borrowed plumes
You try to talk nice,
But we know you are a Jewess.
Stop this stupid game
Don't be rude
There are witnesses here from your childhood.

It was not funny at all and I began to wonder if my idyllic
stay at Mrs. Kałużniacka's was not approaching its end. On
the other hand, it made no sense for a blackmailer to
approach his victim in such an unusual way; it looked rather
as if someone wanted to frighten me. But who and why?
I showed this piece of "poetry" to Cesia and she had no
doubts about its authorship. She recognized in it the style
of Anda, her future sister-in-law, who liked to write
"poems" on different occasions. She was also the only other
person among my former schoolmates who knew my current address. Cesia thought that Anda had sent the threat-
ening lines because she was jealous of Cesia's friendship
with me.

But Anda was a coward, Cesia told me. She would never
have risked making friends with me if I was hunted and
outlawed. "She also remembers," Cesia said, "that you
were the best student, a 'star' in the school. She always
had literary ambitions and could not stand it that your essay
on contemporary Polish poetry was considered one of the
best ever written by a student there."

Cesia was sure that there was nothing to worry about,

that the "poem" was intended only to scare me. But she also told Anda that she knew about the anonymous letter I had received and hinted that she knew who the author was. Cesia was right; there were no more "poems," or any other malicious jokes at my expense.

However, I recalled that petty jealousy and envy had triggered a hostile act against me before. They had prompted Danka's friend Bożena to denounce me to the Kriminal Polizei. Anti-Semitism has always had its roots in religion, politics, and economics, but its manifestations sometimes reflect purely individual prejudices and grudges. The old habit of scapegoating—focusing personal grievances on Jews—was now repeated in my own experience.

Next I was caught up with Helena in a terrible situation. Helena's boyfriend, Stefan, had moved in with us. She had told our landladies that he was her brother, so that they would permit this arrangement. But soon afterward we received a blow: Stefan had been arrested by the Germans, apparently for his involvement in anti-German acts. Helena and the Peasant Battalions found someone who had good connections with the Germans and who promised to help arrange for Stefan's release for an astronomical sum. The money had to be paid in a very short time. The underground was willing to pay it, but they needed time to collect such a huge amount. Again, I went to Cesia for help. My idea was to borrow from the dealers in hard currency who operated in Kercelak, the flea market near the store where Cesia worked. Max, the head of the currency ring, had confidence in us from the time Cesia and I had sold black-market goods on consignment, and he promised to bring the money as quickly as he could raise it. Unfortunately, it was not fast enough: the Germans had

deported Stefan to a concentration camp and had executed
him.

Helena's grief was immense. It was probably made all
the more acute by the hope she had nourished that she
could rescue him, and then the despair she felt in having
failed to do so because of the delay in delivering the ransom. She tried to conceal her pain and became even more
active in the underground. Neither our landladies nor I
tried to console her. We never mentioned Stefan's name
in her presence. I think that she found some comfort in
our love for her. Ten years would pass before Helena
married.

"Tadeusz Is Lost"

IT HAPPENS that people who have just exchanged their first glance and spoken only a few words come to establish bonds of unforeseeable importance. So it was with my casual acquaintance, Tadeusz Dąbrowski.

Shortly after I moved into his godmother's house, he paid a visit to see how things were working out in the new household. His visits became more frequent, and it was obvious that he was interested in me, as I was in him. Mrs. Kałużniacka and Miss Janina gave their blessing to our developing friendship. Both were childless and loved Tadeusz as their own son. As for me, they believed that Tadeusz "could not choose better." I was considered a member of the family.

Tadeusz looked younger than his twenty-five years. He was of medium height and slim. His open face and sky-blue gaze expressed innocence. He was so generous and so deeply honest that he never seemed to suspect others of being otherwise, and at times this childlike trust in people irritated me. I believe it would have taken him a long time to overcome his shyness in the presence of a young woman had we not met on his home ground. He was so unaware of his charms that he could not get over what he considered his good luck in meeting me.

Before long he was waiting for me every day outside the apartment houses where I taught my students. When the lesson was over, we would go to a café for a cup of ersatz coffee. Then he would wait with me until my streetcar came.

As our friendship deepened, Tadeusz confided to me that he was active in the Home Army. But I did not tell him my own secret. He might have been so protective as to call attention to us both had he known how often I was exposed to danger. I would have taken more pleasure in playing my role had I not known that Tadeusz was easily deceived.

Several times I succeeded in persuading him to let me carry his gun, overcoming his objections by reminding him that women were searched less often than men during roundups. And besides, I told him, this was my small contribution to the underground army.

He told me everything about his family, although I knew some details already from Mrs. Kałużniacka. Before the war his father had been active in the cooperative movement, which had played a major role in helping small farmers and small businesses, primarily in the countryside. Later, after the war began, he bought the stationery store on Wilcza Street where I had first met Tadeusz. His mother had worked in the same bank as Mrs. Kałużniacka. Tadeusz's brother had been sent to Auschwitz for anti-Nazi activities and had died there in 1942.

Of course, Tadeusz told his parents about me. They also heard about me from Mrs. Kałużniacka, who was his mother's closest friend. The Dąbrowskis welcomed me cordially and one day invited me to dinner. Over a meal that was remarkably good for the times, we talked about the war. At some point Halina, Tadeusz's older sister, said, "We have to admit that there is one thing we should be grateful to Hitler for. He did away with the Jews."

I was shocked. Although I knew that there were Poles who held this view, no one had ever voiced it in my presence. Before I could regain my composure, though, I heard Mr. Dąbrowski shouting. He was furious at his daughter, and his voice broke. He accused her of being as cruel as the Nazis, and threatened her with God's judgment. She probably was indifferent to the moral content of his pronouncement, but the scorn in her father's voice and the vehemence in his eyes left her speechless. Perhaps she had just wanted to see how I would react to her words. I recalled that once Mrs. Kałużniacka had told me Halina had remarked that I looked a little bit Jewish. Mrs. Kałużniacka had rebuked her: "Nowadays one mustn't say things like that. And you, Halina, be careful yourself, because your husband looks a little bit Jewish." I wondered why Mrs. Kałużniacka had repeated this conversation to me. Perhaps she, too, suspected my secret and wanted to warn me about Halina.

Mr. Dąbrowski managed to calm down, but went on talking. He spoke of the Jews with whom he had worked before the war: how upright and honest, how intelligent, what good friends they had been—always ready to help.

While his words brought relief, I resented deeply the context in which they were spoken. Was it necessary to compliment the victims of Nazi crime? Did any human being ever deserve such a fate?

Mr. Dąbrowski paused, then said, "Yet, for the sake of accuracy, I have to add: although those Jews were otherwise worthy of the highest respect, I never encountered a cultured and refined man among them."

The next day, Tadeusz came to see me, excited about his father's approval of me. "You know, my father said that he had never met such a cultured and refined young lady." The irony of this disgusted me—the approbation expressed so soon after the allegation of Jewish limitations. For a moment, I was determined to tell Tadeusz exactly who I was. The moment passed, though, and I asked him to leave me alone.

Because it never crossed his mind that I was Jewish, Tadeusz was sometimes puzzled by my opinions. "Sometimes you have such strange, almost non-Polish views," he once said after I told him that I expected the Soviets would liberate Poland. On a similar occasion, my friend Cesia had said the same thing—almost in the same words. But she immediately apologized for labeling my political views "non-Polish." She knew I was deeply devoted to Poland and Polish culture, but she also understood that for Jews the next hour might bring death, and that was why we were counting on the Russians. They would arrive ahead of the Western Allies, most of us thought.

I cannot deny that there was a practical side to my friendship with Tadeusz. I imagined that my face would take on something of his typically Polish features and that his company on the street would give me some security. And while I never let him know that I was Jewish, I took great pleasure in having such a devoted friend. Like every young girl, I thrived in an atmosphere of love and admiration. My feelings toward him were complex and at times puzzled me. We were so different in so many respects. He was not a great reader at all; I swallowed up books. He liked operettas; I liked classical music. We saw the world through completely different eyes: he was conservative in his political views, and I wanted to change the social order of the world; he was deeply committed to Catholicism, and I was a non-believer. Yet in spite of these important differences, I grew attached to him. I felt within myself a strange mixture of calculation and emotion, a blending of self-interest with genuine liking in a way I had never before experienced.

What I offered him was true friendship. I was not able to return his love. About this, I did not lie to him. I made it clear that I was not ready to reciprocate his feelings. Not yet, anyway. When he asked me why, I told him the story of Stefan Fisher, my boyfriend in the ghetto. The story was a mixture of truth and half-truth. I never mentioned the Jewish name Fisher. Nor did I tell Tadeusz that Stefan had been killed in the gas chambers of Treblinka. Instead, I invented different circumstances, knowing that I was robbing Stefan of the last hour of his Jewish death. This sad, romantic story was meant to explain my inability to reciprocate Tadeusz's love. But I must also admit that it was his tenderness that enabled me to disclose these emotions which had been long suppressed and deeply concealed.

Poor Tadeusz! He cherished the hope that time would heal my wounds. I pitied him. Sometimes I used to think

about what I would tell him after the war; I rehearsed the
agony of telling him the truth. At other times, I would
imagine a comedy of magnanimity: I would marry him out
of gratitude. I knew it would never happen. Yet the
"drama," with myself the sole audience, somehow allayed
my remorse. As it happened, I never had to tell Tadeusz
the truth. The Germans spared me the necessity.

It was the middle of October 1943. I was at the apartment of one of my students, Lilka, on Złota Street. She
did not attend the underground courses because she was
too far behind the other students. I was expected to de-
velop her interest in studying and her ability to concentrate, while teaching her the full high-school program.
Although I had forgotten much of what I had once learned,
I even managed to teach her some subjects I had never
studied before, such as the Catholic catechism. I kept the
teaching manuals open on the table and read ahead, lec-
turing, explaining as we went along.

Lilka made my job tougher by trying to divert my attention with tales about her "hits" with young men. Usually
I did not let her get away with this: I was paid well by her
parents and took my job seriously. But this time, toward
the end of the three-hour lesson, I was so exhausted that
all I could think of was leaving Lilka and meeting Tadeusz,
who would be waiting to pick me up downstairs. When
the time finally came, however, he was not there. I waited
as long as I could. It was getting late, and I caught the
streetcar in time to reach home before the curfew. I was
disappointed, but also puzzled—Tadeusz never missed a
date.

It was six o'clock in the morning when the bell rang.
One of my landladies opened the door. I jumped out of

my bed and heard Mr. Dąbrowski's broken voice. "Tadeusz is lost."

I ran downstairs. Mr. Dąbrowski told us that the Gestapo had entered the store the previous day and had arrested Tadeusz.

Torn between hope and despair, we waited for news. About two weeks passed. On October 28, I left home to give one of my lessons. As I got off the streetcar, I noticed a group of people gathered in front of a red poster displayed on a town wall. These official announcements appeared almost daily and contained lists of Polish hostages who had been executed. This was the German Army's retaliation for the killing of a German or for acts of sabotage carried out by Polish "bandits," as the Germans used to call members of the underground. When the "bandits" were not caught, the hostages—Poles suspected of underground activities or simply picked up at random—were killed instead.

I cast a glance at the poster and saw the name at once: Tadeusz Dąbrowski. I stood stone-dead, but my face undoubtedly betrayed my feelings. "Brother?" someone asked. "Husband?" I did not answer. Time stood still. It was October 28—ironically, Tadeusz's name day.

A few days later, Mrs. Kałużniacka and I went to see Tadeusz's parents. Miss Janina refused to go with us. She said that she had to watch the house. We knew this was a pretext, that she was afraid to face the bereaved parents. Tadeusz's brother had died in Auschwitz; in three years of war they had lost both their sons. Mr. and Mrs. Dąbrowski welcomed us warmly and with complete composure talked about Tadeusz. They did not know where he had been killed. The Germans used to blindfold and probably drug the hostages before they executed them in different parts of the city. Nobody knew where a particular person was killed. Neighbors would hear shots and then see bloodstains on sidewalks and buildings. Later, people would mark these places with flowers and lighted candles.

Tadeusz's father asked me into another room and gave me the red poster, dated October 28, 1943. He had managed to remove it from a town wall. "I consider you my daughter," he said. "And I am very grateful to you. Tadeusz was so happy after he met you: he often sang the aria 'Oh, Halino . . . My One and Only' [from Bronisław Moniuszko's opera *Halka*]." Tadeusz's father smiled. "Thank you, Zofia."

From time to time, even now, I am overwhelmed by a desire to talk to Tadeusz. I feel there is something I should have said to him.

Devil's Brew

TADEUSZ DROPPED OUT of my life like so many others before him. It even seemed in the nature of things. The long struggle, the persistent suffering, made the losses seem natural. Only now there was no Tadeusz waiting for me in front of my students' houses, no Tadeusz to protect and cherish me. I continued my daily routine; I functioned almost automatically. That was the way it was meant to be, I told myself.

On one of those dull days, I entered a store to make a telephone call. I asked to talk to a friend, referring to him only by his first name. The general rule of conspiracy was to avoid mentioning surnames. In Poland, however, where people mainly used surnames on such occasions, the very adherence to this rule could arouse suspicion.

I sensed I was being watched. After I finished my call,

the customer who seemed to be observing me followed me out of the store. He bowed gallantly, introduced himself as Mr. Mieczysław Pankowski, and asked whether he might accompany me for a while. I replied that I was in a hurry and did not like being addressed by strangers on the street.

"Is it on principle?" he asked. "Or perhaps you are afraid because you are Jewish." Without letting me answer, he fervently assured me that I had nothing to be afraid of, that he had the best intentions, and that he had always had many Jewish friends and missed them keenly—especially Jewesses, who were so intelligent and charming.

His words disgusted and frightened me. Still, his eyes seemed surprisingly friendly. I could not figure him out. Was it blackmail? Or was he telling the truth? He seemed to read my thoughts. "I am not going to blackmail you, as you certainly suspect. Believe me! And think how helpful it would be to make friends with a courageous and intelligent Pole." Then he offered a "scenario" to convince me that he could be trusted. He was going to leave me alone. Certainly I would change streetcars several times to make sure that I was not being followed. Yet, he said, I would be nervous and puzzled. He did not let me interrupt him. He took from his pocket a calling card which gave me his name, address, and telephone number.

"I live with my older sister in a one-family house in the suburbs. It is beautiful and quiet. Take the card." Since I was anxious to get rid of him, I took the card and laughed. He laughed, too. We shook hands. His attentive brown eyes appraised me, as if to read from my face whether I dared to meet his challenge.

I reached home safely, although I was as nervous and

puzzled as my new acquaintance had foreseen. I should have forgotten this episode and thanked God that there had been no blackmail attempt, but my loneliness made me restless. I recalled Pankowski's contagious laugh. I wanted to laugh again, lightheartedly. He would not harm me; he had already had that opportunity. I told my friends Marysia and Celinka about the new acquaintance. "Surely you won't call him," Celinka said to me. She knew my disposition for courting danger. "For God's sake, don't look for trouble."

I decided not to accept the mysterious stranger's invitation. Then, one rainy Sunday, I passed a pharmacy, and found myself calling him. He was delighted and urged me to come at once: "My sister will serve an excellent strong tea and there is a freshly baked poppyseed cake."

Pankowski, beaming, opened the door. The living room was well furnished, and its low ceiling made it feel cozy. I was seated at a small table by the window. Pankowski's sister, the middle-aged widow of an Army officer, brought the tea and cake. Pankowski used every opportunity to compliment me for my courage. I laughed and neither confirmed nor denied his allegation that I was Jewish. I relaxed, objecting only to his opinion that Jewish girls were more intelligent than Polish girls. (I usually smelled the anti-Semitism behind such philo-Semitic remarks.) In this peaceful atmosphere I anticipated a pleasant afternoon.

Quite unexpectedly, Pankowski took my hand and looked into my eyes. A smile crinkled the corners of his eyes. He said softly, "Yet, my charming and smart young lady, you made a mistake, quite a big mistake. When I saw through the window that you really were coming, I made a phone call to the Gestapo to inform them that there is a Jewess in my house. They will arrive soon to pick you up."

My stomach turned. I became numb. It couldn't be true; this would be the most idiotic way to perish. I cast a glance out the window to see if there was a Gestapo car in view, and then turned to Pankowski. He was watching me intently, playing me like a fish at the end of his line. It must be a joke, a nasty joke, I said to myself. But if it is not? I must persuade him to let me escape.

"It is a very improper and stupid joke," I said, putting another piece of poppyseed cake on my plate. I was collected, matter-of-fact. "Suppose," I continued, "that I am Jewish, which you seem strongly to believe. So, what do you want? You want to see me beg for my life? Anyone with a weak heart," I went on, "would have had a heart attack."

Pankowski was delighted. He bowed low to me and kissed my hand. I withdrew it. "Of course it was a joke! You are a wonderful girl. *Chapeau bas*," he added, and made a gesture as if to doff his hat. He took two glasses and a bottle of vodka from a sideboard.

He saw how angry I was. "You were certainly right—my joke was rather uncalled for. But I was so eager to know how you would react." He told me that he was particularly interested in psychology and liked small experiments to test human nature. It was his hobby. He was delighted that this experiment had been such a success.

I was hardly satisfied with his explanations, or with his compliments. I emptied the glass of vodka in one gulp as Poles used to do. It was *bimber*, illegally distilled liquor produced by Pankowski and his sister in their cellar and sold to earn their livelihood during the occupation. The moonshine was very strong. Perhaps treating me to this strong drink was also part of Pankowski's test, since Jews were considered poor drinkers. If so, I passed it successfully. Besides, at that moment I needed the vodka very much. My tension eased.

At least I knew that I was not going to be murdered shortly by the Gestapo. It was "only" a joke. But I was furious at Pankowski. How dare he treat me as a guinea pig to satisfy his hobby, his "curiosity about human nature"! It was almost like the "medical" experiments performed by German physicians on prisoners in the concentration camps.

Pankowski clearly felt that he had gone too far. He begged me to forgive him and to forget the incident. "But please don't forget me or fail to visit me again." I thought him a scoundrel. You will never see me again, I said to myself. Although I felt degraded and hated him, I mainly blamed myself for being so easily lured into a situation that was avoidable. Hadn't I been exposed to enough unavoidable troubles? I finished my tea and cake, enjoyed another glass of vodka, and left.

Several weeks passed. When one student, Lilka, left for the countryside and another passed his exams, I lost a significant part of my meager earnings. When I could find no other source of income, my financial situation became desperate.

I recalled that Pankowski had offered me a job bottling the moonshine he produced and selling it at a nice commission. As much as I disliked him, I had at least to consider the offer. Although I had no flair for selling, I would not mind bottling the liquor. Why not? I would not have to see Pankowski socially, and I needed money. I called up my prospective employer. He was again delighted to hear my voice. I was invited to come the next Sunday.

When I arrived, I noticed the table was set for five. There were vodka glasses, kielbasa, and pickles—a typical Polish snack served with alcohol. "I hope you will not mind my inviting two buddies of mine," he said. He explained that his buddies, in fact, were his business partners. One delivered the potatoes from which the moonshine was produced; the other was a wholesale dealer in vodka. He said they were not exactly "my sort," although they had been university students before the war. With an impudent grin he suggested that I would hardly consider bottle filling proper work for an intellectual. Then he warned me to be careful: he knew only of the business his partners did with him. "Who knows what prewar students may be up to in wartime?" he said.

The two men arrived late and settled right down to the vodka. Pankowski, his sister, and I were good drinkers, but it was impossible to keep up with them. The kielbasa vanished from the table in no time. Only some pickles remained. The Pankowskis had a barrel full of them, and the sister took care to replenish the empty tray. Although the men watched to see that Pankowski's sister and I were served every round of drinks, occasionally I managed, with Pankowski's help, to skip one. Still, I drank a lot and it is still a puzzle how my body could tolerate that much alcohol. At first the men talked business: the price of potatoes, the price of moonshine, the means of transportation, and so on. Pankowski assured his guests that I could be trusted and that they could talk freely. They did.

Nothing loosens the tongue like alcohol, and after a while they switched from talking business to telling jokes—loathsome, dirty jokes. They also bragged about their erotic conquests, until Pankowski felt it necessary to restrain them: "Gentlemen, don't forget, ladies are present."

To my horror, they changed the subject again, this time to the Jews, a popular topic in some Polish circles. The men indicated that they didn't deal with Jews; that is to say, professionally. They used the Polish word *Żydki* (little Jews), which conveys contempt or indulgence mixed with a kind of sympathy. How amazing it is, they said, that those *Żydki* would simply force money on their "protectors," as they referred to themselves. One need only know how to approach Jews: gently and convincingly.

I felt a knot in the pit of my stomach. I was drinking vodka with blackmailers. Pankowski seemed genuinely interested in the course the conversation had taken. Was this due to his passion for studying human behavior? Or did he consider it advantageous to know the dossiers of his business partners? Had he suspected before what their additional source of income was? Was he also amused to watch me and see how I reacted to their confidences?

We learned that the two men specialized in blackmailing their old university classmates. The word "blackmail" was never used. They said they were "protectors" of the Jews, helping the "needy ones." "You would not believe that there are Jews who really don't have money," one said. They saw their blackmail transactions as a kind of "justice." The poor were, so to speak, tax exempt: "Let the rich pay." They even invented a special term for those payments— "Jewish dividends." Their general opinion of the Jews was low: Contrary to popular belief, Jews were foolish. They didn't have the gumption for business and were easy to outwit. Pankowski felt it necessary to interrupt only once, when they started to tell a story about a pretty Jewish girl who had no money. "It was really a pleasure . . ." But they had to stop. "I remind you, ladies are present," Pankowski said.

Pankowski, still chuckling at their stories, took advantage of the pause to ask his guests whether they were ever afraid of being denounced by the Jews after the war. They simply laughed. One raised his hand and enumerated the reasons why they felt entirely safe.

"Pankowski, don't be childish. First," he said, raising a finger, "how many of those wretched Jews will survive? Second"—raising a second finger—"we help them. I personally gave a hundred zlotys to a Jew who had been stripped of everything he had possessed. I even gave him a pack of cigarettes, too. Third, there are means of protecting ourselves. Some of our Jewish classmates happened to reveal the names of their Jewish friends who still possess valuables. Would they like to be reminded of this?" This was followed by another round of vodka. "Cheers!"

Tobacco smoke choked the room. I stopped listening; I was nauseated. Was it because of the vodka? Or was it because of the witches' sabbath I was witnessing? Nobody paid attention to me; they were drunk. Only Pankowski tried to squeeze my hand under the table to show me how he admired my self-possession. I hated him.

It was very late. Without excusing myself, I left the company and went to his sister's room. She followed me. "Had enough vodka?"

"Yes," I said, "and enough of everything, including your little brother." I lay down on a couch. I knew that I was covered by a blanket, and I savored the rest and the warmth—but at the same time I felt I was still in the dining room, now dancing the cancan on the table, breaking glasses and plates. A man with a black beard who looked like Mephistopheles shouted: *"Żydki*, don't be foolish. *Żydki entloyf.* Run away, little Jews!" I woke up. I knew I would never forget the dream.

I refused the breakfast that Pankowski's sister offered me. I refused the tea. "You can't leave like that after a night of drinking."

"I can," I replied, and left hurriedly in the rain-sodden morning, never to return.

My Priests

THE EXPERIENCES of the last several months were exhausting. I found a kind of fatalism settling within me. My friend Helena thought that malnutrition was contributing to my poor health and low spirits. After my unfortunate experience in pursuing a "bottle-filling career," I found I had neither the will nor the stomach to look for another job.

Fortunately, Helena took over for me and soon learned of a teaching position at the Congregation of Saint Francis de Sales. The Salesians were looking for someone to teach accounting. They devoted themselves to caring for neglected children and to teaching various trades, but they also employed laymen to train their priests.

The fathers liked my qualifications: I was a graduate of the Academy of Commerce in Cracow and had a law degree from the Jagiellonian University (the Alma Mater of the future Pope John Paul II). Luckily, I was given the job without having to show my credentials, which were issued, of course, in my Jewish name. Mrs. Uklejska gave me a written testimonial and this satisfied the priests. I would meet my seminarians twice a week in the Salesians' building on Lipowa Street. It was in a section of the city inhabited mostly by the poor. It was also frequented by thieves and other shady characters. The priests had probably chosen this neighborhood so as to care for the children of disadvantaged families.

At first our meetings were formal and devoted exclusively to study. But soon we all became friends, and I stayed longer than the time allotted for the lesson, discussing politics and other topics. The priests, who were well informed, shared their news with me. They kept a hidden radio—its discovery by the Germans would have meant severe punishment—and had wide access to the underground press. They also discussed with me their plans for after the war: they wanted to help undo the damage done by the Nazis in the education and morals of Polish youth. Their mission was very much in the spirit of the order, which was founded in 1859 by a young Italian priest, Don Bosco, primarily for the care of needy young people.

I liked my work. The priests were responsive, modest, and unusually diligent. I was also well paid. Most of all, I found it extraordinary that I, a Jew, was teaching Catholic priests—an arrangement virtually unheard of in Poland. Sometimes I wondered whether they suspected that I was Jewish.

A few weeks after I started teaching, my friend Celinka

told me that an acquaintance of hers was looking for shelter for a Jewish child. I promised to ask my students whether they could help. At the risk of betraying myself, I spoke about the problem to one of the priests after a lesson. He was not at all surprised. It would be difficult, he said, but he would discuss it with the Father Superior. I would have an answer by our next lesson.

The next lesson was not to be. On the appointed day, while walking toward the Salesian building, I heard a "Psst"—a warning given by strangers in the streets of Warsaw when a roundup was imminent. I stopped and walked quickly in the opposite direction. Later I learned that the SS had surrounded the building and arrested several priests, interning them in Auschwitz and other concentration camps. I also heard that several Salesian priests had been executed.

Years later, in the United States, I discovered more about the fate of my students. The Reverend Arthur Słomka, a priest of Polish origin who worked at a school run by the Salesian fathers in Ramsey, New Jersey, sent me the monumental work *Martyrology of the Polish Roman-Catholic Priesthood under the Hitlerian Occupation from 1939 to 1945*, by the Reverend Wictor Jacewicz in cooperation with the late Reverend Jan Woś. Although the book documented the suffering of many Polish priests, I did not find any information about the Lipowa Street Salesians. I wrote to the author in Poland; after more than two months of inquiries, he was able not only to find one of my students, the Reverend Julian Rykała, but also to include in his answer—to my great surprise—a letter from him. Father Rykała's letter was warm and expressed his happiness that I had survived. He wrote that after their arrest the priests were much concerned about my fate. They wondered whether I had been trapped in the roundup on my way to the lesson. They also worried that my fee for the lessons had not been paid. Their concern for me at a time when they were threatened with death was touching.

Father Rykała is now a priest in Wyżne, a village in southern Poland, not far from Rzeszów. From time to time we exchange letters and holiday wishes. He has written to me with news of my other students, and once sent me his memoirs, *The Prisoners* (*Więzniowie: Heftlingi Emigranci*), a small book describing the period from his arrest until his liberation from a concentration camp.

It was midnight of February 7, 1944, when German cars first surrounded the building. Inside were twenty priests and several dozen students. The SS searched every corner and took whatever seemed of value. They found no evidence of anti-German activities, yet they threatened to shoot the priests on the spot. Suddenly the sound of an organ was heard. The church had been locked, and the priests had been ordered to stay in the courtyard. Who could it be? It was a German soldier attempting to display his talents—while only a few feet away, hidden behind the organ, was one of my students, the Reverend Stanisław Burzynski. He managed to escape, but thirteen others were taken to the Pawiak, the notorious prison for political offenders. They never found out why they had been arrested. Had they been denounced? Did the Germans hate their charitable work? Or was it a tactic of terror?

Father Rykała and several other priests were later transported from one concentration camp to another. Father Rykała was imprisoned in Gross-Rosen, Dora, Osterode, and Wattenstedt. Virtually starving, and forced to do work—digging in quarries, grubbing in forests—that was far too strenuous for him, he developed tuberculosis. Still, he and five of my other students survived.

Only the Reverend Stefan Wojciechowski died in the camp. He was a quiet man, always concerned about others, always ready to share a portion of food with his hungry fellow prisoners. He was sick and utterly exhausted. In Gross-Rosen, two kapos named Schultz and Max took a sadistic pleasure in bullying him. Father Rykała saw him for the last time in March 1945. He was dying. "The only thing that could have been done for him," Father Rykała writes, "would have been to give him even the smallest bit of food. I had nothing at all." Father Wojciechowski, together with other terminally ill prisoners, was transported from the concentration camp in Dora to the one in Hazelhausen. Nobody ever heard from him again. To the list of my losses, another name was added.

The Child in the
Parish House

HELENA BRODOWSKA was a genius in emergencies. She knew that I desperately needed to earn a living, and she soon learned of another teaching job, this time in Ryki. It was to be the setting of my most moving encounter with members of the Polish priesthood.

Ryki, then a small town of four or five thousand inhabitants, is situated halfway between Warsaw and Lublin. The cooperative movement, which had been well organized in Poland before the war, had established numerous cooperatives and schools in the towns and villages, including Ryki.

The high school in Ryki had been shut down, since the Germans allowed only elementary-level education. The former teachers, nonetheless, were able to get permission from the Lublin Schulrat, the German educational office, to train salesmen and clerks for rural commune stores. Under this guise, they hoped to provide young people with a high-school education. The school would follow the tradition of Polish "folk universities," which offered a variety of courses to workers and peasants, without the formal requirements of regular universities. The programs were flexible and responded to the various needs of their students.

It was clear that we would not be permitted to teach the Polish language or Polish history. But we could smuggle many things into the curriculum. For example, the teacher who was to explain how to organize a rural store managed to lecture on the history of the cooperative movement, and I, who was to teach bookkeeping and commercial arithmetic, managed to lecture on economic history and political geography. Of all my teaching jobs, none had been— or ever would be—as exciting as this one. I would never again meet young people with such a hunger for knowledge. They were a grateful audience. Some of my students, in their thirties, were older than I. They listened motionless, sometimes openmouthed. There were so many questions to be answered that I could not rest during the breaks. Sometimes we would continue our discussions after class, and then sing folk songs that the students taught me.

To be safe and inconspicuous, we decided to teach not in the school building in Ryki but in a nearby hamlet, Sobieszyn. Students would go there from Ryki and a number of other villages. I lived in the house of a peasant, who gave me his best room. I had a desk, armchairs, and a couch. It was the kind of furniture rarely found in the countryside in those days. I could not rid myself of the suspicion that it was "post-Jewish property," which meant that it had been stolen from Jews or bought from looters. I did not like the family I stayed with, although they fed me generously with as much milk, eggs, and cheese as I could want. For the first time in four years, I had enough food.

The first Sunday after our course began, all the teachers were invited to the parish priest's house for afternoon tea. Although most of us were atheists, we accepted the invitation; it was customary for newcomers in small parishes to visit the local priest. For myself, the visit had a special meaning. For the first time in my life, I was going to meet a priest socially.

The Reverend Alexander Zalski was a tall, somewhat bulky man in his forties. Although he was kind, good-humored, and hospitable, my fellow teachers—young intellectuals—immediately attacked his theological beliefs, taking full advantage of his lack of argumentative skills. Not even the delicious tea and the cherry cake baked by the priest's housekeeper could temper their zeal. I felt sorry for him; in that company he was a minority of one.

Suddenly we heard a child crying, "Father! Father!" A girl, about four or five years old, ran into the room. I had rarely seen a child of such beauty and natural grace. Her curly hair and eyes were raven-black. Her complexion was dark. There could be no doubt that she was Jewish. I was startled by her presence in the priest's home.

The next moment she was in his arms. Still sobbing and out of breath, she reminded him to tell the story he always told her at mealtimes. "Father" is the term by which people usually address a priest, but I felt that this child actually considered him her protector, as she would have looked on her own father. Later I would see how he fed her, comforted her, and stayed by her bedside until she fell asleep.

During our first visit, Father Zalski seemed slightly embarrassed by the little intruder, but he did not reprove her. Solemnly he promised to tell the story later, and Marianna, happy and reassured, left the room. Afterward, he mumbled a few words of apology. Although as a priest he had no experience in raising children, he said, he had undertaken to care for this child because her parents, both dead, had been distantly related to him.

Did he realize that we knew the girl was Jewish? Was he alarmed because we had seen her? I do not think so. It seemed inconceivable that he would fear that we would denounce him. Besides, her presence at the parish must have been widely known; one could not keep such a secret in a small village.

We became frequent guests of Father Zalski, and my fellow teachers learned to restrain their theological attacks. He was impressed by our affiliation with the cooperative movement, and to let him know that he was fully accepted by our group, we would address him as Colleague and Priest Zalski. The term "colleague" was often used by members of the cooperative movement, as the term "comrade" was used among socialists.

I deeply admired Father Zalski's devotion to the Jewish child and his courage in harboring her. His risk was great, for the punishment meted out by the Nazis was merciless. I personally knew of seven Sisters of Charity at the orphanage of Saint Stanislaus in Warsaw who were executed for hiding Jewish children. I had also heard that many nuns were blackmailed. The Polish priests were widely engaged in helping Jews. This was but a part of their activities in the Resistance for which they were subsequently persecuted by the Nazis. More than 4,400 Catholic priests and brothers were put into concentration camps, where half of them were killed. Of 1,100 nuns imprisoned in concentration camps, about 240 perished.

I regretted that I never had the opportunity to express my feelings to Father Zalski, but the Jewish child was not a topic to be discussed then. Unfortunately, our teaching program did not last long. Someone from the Schulrat hinted that the German authorities had learned about our illegal activities and were going to do away with the course. Zofia Glazer-Olszakowska, at the time the principal of the school, said we owed this information—as well as our rescue—to an officer from Vienna. The lady of the local manor, in whose home he lived, persuaded him to use his influence on behalf of the teachers and students. Still, our arrest seemed only postponed, and we took prompt action. Under the pretext that our students needed practical training, we sent them to various rural cooperatives—we had friends everywhere—and then left the village.

Only recently I learned about the fate of Father Zalski and the child. Father Zalski stayed in his parish until his death in the 1960s. Little Marianna, whose real name was Rachela, survived. Her mother had taken poison in Siedlce during the deportation action. An old school friend of her mother's had rescued the child. Later, after being passed from hand to hand, she was entrusted to Father Zalski's care. In 1946, with the help of Mrs. Glazer-Olszakowska, Marianna was sent to an uncle in Israel and was brought up in a kibbutz there. Eventually, she studied economics, married, and had two children. Mrs. Glazer-Olszakowska visited her in Israel and reported that she had become a highly respected civil servant. I never saw her after that early spring of 1944 in Father Zalski's parish house in Sobieszyn. I am happy that she survived.

The Polish Policeman

I RETURNED to my landladies in Warsaw. After all the
tension I had felt during the last weeks in Sobieszyn, I was
now beginning to relax. My resistance had been strengthened by my satisfaction in teaching there and by the pleasure of working with my fellow teachers and our grateful
students. The good food also contributed to my health and
spirits. Maybe things were looking up.

One day my landladies and I decided to arrange a small
party for Helena; I don't remember what the occasion was.
I stopped in front of a drugstore at the corner of Marszałkowska and Świętokrzyska Streets to buy a present for
her, perhaps a nice comb and mirror. To check the prices
of the items displayed in the window, I put on my glasses—
something I seldom did because they called attention to
my face.

It was a mistake. In a few minutes I was approached by a young couple. "We want to talk to you," the man said. I knew immediately what they wanted. I waited calmly with a pleasant smile, as if I expected them to ask directions. I even noticed the man's appearance: well dressed, his hair neatly parted, he looked like a hairdresser who charmed his female clients. But certainly he did not intend to charm me. He meant business and got to the point right away. He was a plumber, a Pole who had been called into the ghetto occasionally. He remembered my face. "You are Jewish and you pay," he said.

I started to argue, but I knew it was hopeless. I had in my pocketbook just enough to buy the small gift for Helena—not enough to satisfy the blackmailers. I had at home only a little more. "Don't play games with us," my persecutors said. "Either you pay or we go to the Aleja Szucha [Gestapo headquarters]." They meant it.

I tried my usual dilatory tactics. I told them that I was ready to go to the Gestapo to teach *them* a lesson. Of course, they didn't believe me. The trip would take a long time, I told them. (Forever, I thought ironically, if I actually did end up at Gestapo headquarters.) First, I said, I wanted to drop in somewhere on Twarda Street, which was about five hundred yards from us. I did not know anyone there, but since I hadn't the slightest idea what to do next, I thought I would try to gain time. I was waiting for a miracle. The blackmailers agreed to go with me. Presumably, they thought I was going somewhere to pick up the money. As we walked together up Marszałkowska Street, we must have looked like three good friends on a stroll, enjoying the mild spring sun.

From about a dozen yards or so, I noticed a Polish policeman. He looked like a nice person, probably in his fifties. Did it matter what he looked like? It was well known that Polish policemen were ruthless with Jews. It was crazy to expect help from him. Even if he didn't join my black-mailers to get his own share of the money, he probably would take me to the police station to check my papers; one telephone call to the vital-records office would be sufficient to find out that I was wanted by the Gestapo.

But I was in a strange state of mind. I was overwhelmed by an anger that was stronger than fear. It was utterly irrational to expect help from a policeman. I should have called my friends; they would probably have found some money to rescue me. I made up my mind quickly—and behaved as if throwing myself to a hungry lion. I began to run toward the policeman. By the time my surprised per-secutors caught up with me, I was talking to him breath-lessly: "These are blackmailers. They say I am Jewish. They want money."

The blackmailers tried to tell their story, but I inter-rupted them constantly. The policeman could hardly get a word into our quick exchange of mutual accusations. As always in such a situation, a crowd gathered. We were, I recall, on Bagno Street, a neighborhood where shadowy transactions thrived. One could get everything there, from safety pins and old sewing-machine parts to hard currency. It was a district of pickpockets, prostitutes, and black-mailers—illegal traffickers in goods and souls—Jewish souls, to be precise.

Although this was exactly the kind of crowd I would have avoided at any cost, it was clear that I now had to appeal to them, convert them, against all odds, into my allies. I decided to brazen it out and to use the street language of my audience—the underworld vocabulary I had acquired during my stay in the neighborhood. I demanded that the blackmailers show their identity cards, but I refused to show mine. "Not in your presence," I said. "I will show my Kennkarte to the officer if requested." I went so far as to take a notebook from my pocketbook and write down the name of the male blackmailer. (The young woman with him had cleared out.) Thus I let the audience assume that if the police did not take action against the blackmailer, I would. This was a hint that I had contacts with the underground, and it was a very risky move. But I knew the psychology of the crowd, and in that atmosphere it was very unlikely that anyone would denounce me. Indeed, my indignation had spread to the spectators; they actually applauded. I continued my oratory: "Even if I were Jewish—whoever I might be—what a shame to cooperate with the Germans."

My listeners—I would bet that there were blackmailers among them—again applauded. They were overcome by my patriotic rhetoric and impressed by my strong language. It did not cross anyone's mind to scrutinize the length of my nose: I was one of them. I was winning, and the setting that at first seemed only to compound my danger was contributing instead to my rescue.

The policeman, silent up to now, said that we'd better get moving; he had no more time to spend listening to us. The blackmailer vanished. The policeman and I started walking slowly in the direction of the Church of All Saints.

"As a matter of fact," he said, "I should have asked you to show me your Kennkarte." I reached for my pocketbook. He shook his head. "But I'm not going to do it," he said. He looked at me in a friendly way, but I read in his eyes: "We both know." "I wish you the best," he said, shaking my hand, and left.

Suddenly, as when I had escaped the blackmailers on the streetcar, I was overcome with a terrible fatigue. I badly needed to rest, but I was afraid I might go to pieces and fail to spot the blackmailers if they returned to follow me. I took a streetcar, another one, then a bus, until I was sure that I was safe. Then I went to see Marysia at the countess's house.

She opened the door and knew immediately that something had happened. For a while I could not tell the story, even to her. She asked the housekeeper to bring me a cup of coffee, telling her the first lie to come to mind—that I had begun to menstruate. (During the war, girls commonly stopped menstruating for long periods because of nerves. This, in fact, had also happened to me.) The housekeeper was very sympathetic, and in no time brought a cup of coffee and helped me to lie down—my legs wouldn't stop shaking. Thanks to the coffee, the rest, and Marysia's affectionate care, I felt better in an hour or so. When I finally told Marysia what had happened, she was more shocked than I had been. How could I have taken such a terrible chance? Didn't I know I was risking my life? I was crazy, she said, to expect help from a Polish policeman. I should have called her or my other friends.

She was right. I should not have done it. But I was happy that I had escaped against all odds. And it was good to feel that one could meet fine human beings when least expected, even in the uniform of a Polish policeman. It strengthened my confidence in the future.

Hopes and Anguish

Soon it seemed all Warsaw was singing a song called "The Red Poppies at Monte Cassino," hastily composed by Alfred Schutz to the words of Feliks Konarski, to celebrate the impressive victories scored on May 18, 1944, by the Second Polish Corps fighting with the Western Allies in Italy. Warsaw was full of enthusiasm.

On June 6, I learned that the Western Allies had landed in Normandy. I had no radio and did not read the newspapers, which would distort or hold back such information anyway. Instead, I found out the news from a passerby on the street. People talked of nothing else. From their mood, one would think the Americans stood at the gates of Warsaw.

Without a thought for the expense, I bought a huge bunch of lilacs from a sidewalk vender to present to Mrs.

Uklejska. At her home, as in many others, this day was celebrated as the holiest of holidays. We drank real tea, ate cake baked especially for the occasion, and talked about the prospect of peace, although we would have another year to wait. After the war, whenever I visited Mrs. Uklejska in June, I would always bring lilacs and we would talk about that great day. And we would have tea and a cake that was no longer made with German ersatz ingredients. But we remembered the taste.

Although one could smell in the air the approaching end of the war, the tiny group of Jews hiding on the Aryan side lived in the same danger as before. It even seemed that the number of blackmail attempts and denunciations increased, as if the scavengers of war wanted to take advantage of the last months of a thriving business. I heard even more anti-Semitic remarks than usual on trolleys and buses, in the streets and in stores. Anti-Semitism was clearly growing among the Polish populace as each day the victorious Soviet Army moved closer to the former Polish–Russian border.[*]

Rumors that the Soviets supported the Jews were widespread and found ready acceptance. They raised fears that there would be bloody retaliation against the Poles by the Jews who served in the Soviet Army, as well as by those

---

[*] In 1943, after most of the Polish Jews had been murdered, the head of the Polish underground organizations advised his superiors in London to restrain their pro-Jewish statements because the country "does not like Jews." Jan Tomasz Gross, *Polish Society under German Occupation: The Generalgouvernement, 1939–1945* (Princeton: Princeton University Press, 1979), pp. 184–85.

This was not the first statement of this kind. In September 1941, the commander of Armia Krajowa, the underground Home Army, reported to the Polish government-in-exile: "Please accept it as a fact that the overwhelming majority of the country is anti-Semitic." Lucy S. Dawidowicz, *The Holocaust and the Historians* (Cambridge, Mass.: Harvard University Press, 1981), p. 93.

who would be liberated by Soviet troops as they moved into Poland. These fears were strongest, obviously, among the murderers and blackmailers. But the possibility of such reprisals did not stop them; in fact, it may have spurred them on.

There were also the people who had appropriated Jewish property, as well as the Poles who had once volunteered to take property for safekeeping from their Jewish friends and neighbors. Maybe they would have to return all these things to their owners. They did not like this prospect. They had become accustomed to these Jewish things and considered them their own. Even those who did not participate in persecuting Jews felt bad when they thought that again the Polish landscape would be polluted by the presence of the Jews. Many had been pleased that the Germans had done the dirty job of making the country *Judenfrei* while their own hands remained clean.

While anti-Semitism was growing, some people were even preparing alibis. One of my neighbors, who probably suspected that I was Jewish, or perhaps wanted a witness, told me how good she had been to the Jews: she had known about one in hiding and had not denounced him to the Germans. She obviously expected that he would be grateful for her generosity.

And I, Zofia Rubinstein, had to listen to such stories; or maybe it was Zofia Sielczak, a "pure" Polish girl, christened in the Church of Saint John at Sowia Street? I had to listen to people I did not even know, people I had just met. With strangers I had to be particularly cautious. The anti-Semitic and anti-Russian feelings were so strong that to express a more favorable view of Jews or Russians was to risk being handed over on the spot to the Germans. If

I happened to get embroiled in such a conversation, I tried to get rid of my "compatriot"—whom I feared and despised—as soon as possible.

I have tried to re-create in my mind the picture of this young girl, myself, as if she were someone else; how, mingling with the crowd, she walked, self-confident, through the streets of Warsaw. She was always smiling as if something pleasant had just happened to her. She carried her head high, and in her hair was a flower. What was going on inside?

I remember how she was possessed by envy toward the people she passed in the street. They were not Jewish. She could not part with her camouflage even for a moment; they could be themselves. She hated herself for being different, not only because of the danger that it posed, but also because she felt a stranger to the place and to the people. This stood in the way of her desire, so natural and human, to belong to the crowd surrounding her—the crowd she sometimes despised for its primitiveness and hated for its cruelty.

My need to belong somewhere was accompanied by a desire to run away from my Jewishness. To achieve these ends, it was not enough to stick a smile on my face or a flower in my hair. It was not enough to make up the most plausible story that could be adapted to the occasion; it was not enough to invent the aunt in Zielonka and fictitious parents, who usually appeared in my story as "long-dead loved ones." It was necessary that I not only assume her role but that I identify with Zofia Sielczak—or at least learn to get used to her. To accomplish this, I had to suppress the image of Zofia Rubinstein, who stubbornly kept emerging from the past. But my past self was not easily subsumed. Many times, childlike, I repeated to my-self, "Zofia Rubinstein is dead; long live Zofia Sielczak!" It did not help.

Belonging to two worlds meant that I did not belong anywhere, that I existed in painful isolation. I did not suc-ceed in creating a whole person from the various indi-viduals whose roles I played successfully in different circumstances. This complicated situation inflicted scars on my character which lasted long after the war; probably some remain to this day. For a long time two Zofias existed: the one who always smiled in the streets, and the other, mourning her losses in solitude; the one complying with Miss Okonska's finicky ways or Danka's whims, and the other, stubborn and independent; the country teacher in Aunt Aniela's concierge quarters, and the graduate of Po-land's finest university. I constantly felt the presence of the two identities, each trying to overwhelm the other. I could not let Zofia Rubinstein prevail. I had to be Zofia Sielczak. It all came down to survival.

*   *   *

It is May 1984, forty years since the events I have just described. I stopped writing for several months in December 1983, when I learned I had cancer. My lymphoma, which originally had been diagnosed as the kind of cancer that developed slowly, turned out to be very aggressive. I was hospitalized four times in four months. Strangely, when I was describing the course of my illness, I subconsciously used the military terminology that had served to describe the Nazi offensive in 1939. I talked about the Blitzkrieg of my lymphoma; it progressed like German hordes; I heard in my head the boots of German soldiers entering my defenseless body the way they trampled the defenseless body of my country; the unbearable ringing in my ears sounded like the obnoxious "Horst Wessel Lied" sung by the German troops. Even the radiation therapy I perceived as the bombing of the tumor in my spinal cord. In my descriptions, my illness appeared as an enemy in German uniform—fast, cruel, and victorious. It was my son-in-law, Henryk, who made me aware of these parallels.

Chemotherapy has made me feel much better, but the doctors cannot predict how long this remission will last. I don't know how much time is left for me to go on writing my memoir. That is why I must hurry, must leave out events I had planned to include. I want to have it finished; I have never liked unfinished work.

It is a lazy afternoon in Salt Lake City, Utah. After I left the Sloan-Kettering Memorial Hospital in New York City, I came here to be with my younger daughter, who is a physician. Today she is working in the hospital. Henryk, a professor of mathematics at the University of Utah, is in his office, probably grading midterm exams. It is very quiet here at home. I am alone—or practically alone, the dog my only company. I am looking out at a lovely little garden. From the other window I see the city below and the Rocky Mountains beyond. In a way, I am reconciled to my present situation. I don't have to fight alone for my survival as I did forty years ago. I am under the excellent care of my daughter and the doctors. Suddenly it crosses my mind that today is May 29. On this very day forty years ago, Tolek, Danka's son, was born.

*　　　*　　　*

The Journey to Freedom

WHEN TOLEK WAS BORN that day in Warsaw, there was nobody to care for Danka but me; she had neither husband nor family. I brought her food—one could not live on the hospital diet then—and flowers, and sent her encouraging letters. (To prevent infection, visitors were not allowed in the maternity wards.)

On the day Danka was discharged from the hospital, it was I who came to pick her up. Danka was radiant, but still very weak. I carried the little boy in my arms. We boarded the streetcar through the front door, which was reserved for Germans, cripples, and mothers with infants. Poles had to use the rear door, which was usually crowded with people pushing to get on. For me, this *nur für Deutsche* entrance had an additional advantage: nobody would scrutinize my face for Jewish features.

When the baby was baptized, I declined the honor of being godmother; I did not want to assume the religious obligations. Danka understood, and instead appointed me his aunt—which is what he calls me to this day.

The summer was hot and very uncomfortable. Danka returned to Radość. I stayed there with her from time to time, usually with Celinka, who took advantage of these visits to practice medicine again. She found Danka slow to recover from childbirth, but Tolek was thriving.

On July 28, 1944, Celinka and I went to Radość, but it was more than a casual trip. There was something in the air of Warsaw that prompted us to leave on that day. Rumors that an uprising was imminent were confirmed by our friends in the underground, but they could not say anything more definite.

Celinka and I left Warsaw with mixed feelings: we assumed that as Jews we might be exposed to additional danger during an uprising. And we were right. Many Jews who believed the insurgents would not hurt them left their hiding places and were killed by those who would use any opportunity to get rid of a Jew. On the other hand, our hatred of the Germans and our desire to fight for the city we loved tempted us to remain. Although the survival instinct prevailed, we still tried to convince ourselves that we would have time to return to Warsaw and to join the insurrection.

Before we left Warsaw, we stopped off at Marysia's and urged her to join us. She wanted to, but refused; she considered it her duty to take care of the old countess. Such loyalty seemed unusual under the circumstances. After all, the countess had her son, and Marysia was not obligated to him. True, the count had been considerate—but the work had still been very difficult. Moreover, Celinka said with the authority of a doctor, the old lady would die very soon. She was right. The countess died a few days later, and the count, after thanking Marysia and the housekeeper in his very polite manner for the excellent job they had done, dismissed them. He had foreseen that food would become a major problem in the city, and although his pantry was well stocked, he saw no reason for sharing his provisions with the devoted nurse and housekeeper. Thus Marysia was left on her own in a time of great turmoil.

Unable to convince Marysia to join us, Celinka and I headed for Radość, where we met Janek. Although the love affair was over, Janek felt that Danka needed moral and material support, and he did what he could for her. He convinced us that we could stay longer in the country and get back to the city at the right moment. He was wrong. On the day we left Warsaw, an official communiqué from Moscow announced that Marshal Konstantin Rokossovky's troops were forty miles from the city. We did not know about this announcement, and Janek left for work the next day on the last train to run from Radość to Warsaw.

On August 1, the insurrection was proclaimed by General T. Bór-Komorowski, commander of the Home Army. All lines of communication with Warsaw were cut off. The city was surrounded by German troops. It seemed that we would have to stay in Radość until the end of the insurrection.

The city fought its desperate battle for more than two months. The Russians halted their offensive, and their troops stopped a few miles outside the city, on the eastern side of the Vistula. Why didn't they move to help the insurgents? There is voluminous literature on this question. Russian and pro-Russian Polish historians have contended that the Russians could not rescue the dying city for strategic reasons. Western historians have maintained that the considerations were strictly political: that the Russians knew that the Home Army, under orders from the Polish émigré government in London, wanted to seize power before the Soviet Army took the Polish capital. The ill-prepared Home Army had called the uprising in haste, without consulting the Russians or the Western Allies. For the Soviets the failure of the uprising was more than convenient. They wanted the hostile Home Army to bleed to death so that the Committee of National Liberation, a provisional government created by the Polish Communists, could take power in the transition period and organize what would become the satellite government of Poland.

The Russians had patience: for sixty-three days they stood on the eastern bank of the Vistula, until the city surrendered to the Germans on October 3. Sixteen thousand insurgents and 159,000 civilians were killed. Thousands of Warsavians were shipped to factories or concentration camps in Germany.

A Midsummer Night's Dream

WE BELIEVED we would have to stay in Radość until the end of the uprising, but after a few days a small unit of the Russian Army appeared in the town. Whether it had become separated from the main forces or was a reconnaissance unit was a matter of no military significance. For us, however, it meant liberation.

When a neighbor ran down the road shouting hysterically, "The Russians are here!" we could not believe it. At first we thought she had gone mad. We ran to our balcony. And there we saw them, the first Russians! Our liberators!

With the Russians now in Radość and the Germans holding their position in Międzylesie, the enemies were separated by about two miles of dense forest. The exchange of artillery fire began almost immediately. A few Russian soldiers entered our house, asking why we were there.

They were friendly and polite, but they advised us to leave Radość at once; it was going to become a battlefield and we might be hurt or killed. Then they began to entrench themselves in our garden.

When our neighbors in the Baptist house across the road were also advised by the Russians to leave, our small party of four was joined by one of them—a man carrying an infant. The mother had been wounded in the first hour of the crossfire, and the Russians had taken her to a military hospital. The baby was unbelievably ugly, even grotesque.

It was hot. The famous August sky—clear and bright—often described in the literature of this period, enabled the German planes to fly low over houses and living targets. We walked through the open fields looking for a village where we could stay awhile and rest. On our way we met more Russian soldiers. Here and there, bombshells burst over our heads.

Danka, Celinka, and I did not react at all to these explosions, but the Russian soldiers, brave veterans of many battles, automatically protected their heads or threw themselves on the ground. We had not developed this reflex. One of the soldiers, surprised that we lacked this natural defense mechanism, asked why we behaved so strangely. His question made us realize that we had been deprived of some part of the natural life instinct. In our minds there was only one threat: the Nazis. We were impervious to the fear of death in any circumstances other than capture by the Germans. For us the war had ended at the very moment we saw the first Russian soldier on Polish soil, though the war was to go on for almost a year and many more people would die.

Our small group—Danka and the child, Celinka and I, and the neighbor with his infant—continued the strenuous walk. Suddenly Tolek began to cry; he was hungry. Danka sat down to nurse Tolek in the shade of the solitary tree we found. Close to her stood the man holding his miserable infant. Danka, in the habit of asking my approval for everything she did, looked at me and said, "You know, I have more milk than I need for Tolek. I think I can also nurse this man's baby." I was expecting this; undoubtedly this was why he had joined our party. When Tolek was fed, the other baby eagerly seized Danka's breast and began to suck.

After we had walked about ten miles to the east, we reached a village named Zanęcin, where we went from one cottage to another, asking in vain for shelter. Finally a poor peasant family agreed to let us stay in a small vacant room, and gave us straw pallets to spread on the floor. Our neighbor found a place nearby, much more comfortable than ours. He had money. The three of us together had about twenty zlotys. Predictably, the peasants demanded exorbitant amounts for everything; they looked forward to accommodating more refugees, who would have to pay whatever they asked.

When it got dark, Celinka and I went to dig out some potatoes; we also found some rotten carrots and other vegetables which the peasants had considered inedible. They tasted good to us. And our neighbor, who seemed to be rolling in money, brought milk and food to Danka, which she insisted on sharing with us.

Half a mile from the village we found a pond where we could bathe, there being no facilities in the cottage. We had to be sparing with the one bar of soap in our possession. But we were to get a windfall: the next day I was given more bars of soap by a Russian major from Leningrad who arrived at the village with his unit.

This was my first close contact with a Russian. There had been no time for conversation with the Russian soldiers in Radość or during our walk to Zanęcin, and the few sentences we did exchange had to depend on the common features of the two Slavic languages. With the Russian major, though, I could speak German—when nobody was around who could suspect us of being German spies or, just as bad, Jews. We spent all night talking under the stars, sitting on a bale of hay in a meadow some distance from the village.

I trusted the major and told him that I was Jewish. I told him what I had gone through during the four years of the war. I spoke of those I had loved and lost. It was so good to talk to him. He talked about his war experiences, but very little about his life before the war. I learned only that he, too, was Jewish, an engineer whose wife and son had perished during the siege of Leningrad. I shared his sorrow, he shared mine. He was very attractive and intelligent. But the most striking thing about him was his sadness. When I tried to talk about the future, he fell silent.

Today, after my experiences in Communist Poland, I can understand why he was so reluctant to talk about the reality of the Soviet Union. He might have foreseen what the Poles and the Jews could expect once the Russians dominated Poland. But he was silent about that. I have reason to believe that he had full confidence in me and was not afraid to reveal what he knew. But keeping quiet on political topics had become a habit for the Russians. Even a joke was dangerous. According to a Russian saying, "Those who told jokes wound up building Belamor," the White Sea canal where, according to Solzhenitsyn, a hundred thousand prisoners died between 1931 and 1933.

It was also possible that my Russian friend did not want to deprive me of hope for my own future and the future of my country.

I would have time to learn.

At dawn we embraced affectionately—two close friends of a midsummer night's dream—knowing we would never meet again. Next day he was to leave Zanęcin and go with the army *na zapad*, westward, to Berlin. There they would "crush the beast in his own lair," to use Stalin's famous words. I returned to our cottage with even more of a desire to take part in "crushing the beast." The major had told me that the Polish Army was in Lublin, so now Celinka and I had no reason to stay in Zanęcin. We wanted to join the Polish Army and fight the Nazis.

But we could not take Danka and the baby with us; they could not walk all the way to Lublin. Danka was still nursing the neighbor's child and he was giving her food. He could scarcely conceal the animosity he felt toward Celinka and me. He suspected—correctly—that Danka shared his food with us; although he had a lot of money, he did not like feeding anyone but the woman he needed to nurse his child. He urged us to leave. Danka agreed; under the circumstances, we could do nothing for her. She felt sure that the man would continue to help her. He would not risk giving cow's milk to his child: many cows were tubercular. Although the three of us believed that we would meet again very soon, we cried when we said goodbye. At the same time, we were very happy to leave, and sure that Danka would be taken care of. We could not have known that she would soon be abandoned and that we would not find her until after the war ended eight months later.

The First Warning Signs

THE ROAD TO LUBLIN was jammed with Russian trucks and civilians and wanderers who refused to settle down until they had seen how the arrival of the new rulers, the Russians and their Polish followers, would affect their lives. Celinka and I had no doubts. Every step brought us closer to our goal—reaching the Polish Army in Lublin and joining its ranks. We felt so light we were almost flying. How could one be tired when the goal was so splendid?

We spotted a Jewish couple among the crowd. Their pale faces betrayed the many months they must have spent in hiding, deprived of daylight. In their eyes uncertainty and fear still lingered. It seemed to me that I caught a sign of recognition when they looked in our direction. Although our faces, as well as our tanned skin, did not betray us so easily, nevertheless they could have realized we were

Jews. And I felt that even if they had not recognized us, I ought to have responded immediately, because they were persecuted, confused, strangers even to light and air. They certainly were unable to make the first move. I should have been the first to stretch out my hands or to throw myself into *their* arms. Weren't they *my* people?

But I refused to acknowledge them. The mere remembrance of this episode brings the deepest shame; I have never experienced anything similar. I betrayed them—more, I betrayed myself. I avoided making eye contact, any contact. I pretended not to notice them. For a long time afterward I suffered from an obsessive fear that unexpectedly I would meet my fellow Jewish travelers from the road to Lublin. This time I would recognize them. I would confess and ask forgiveness. Would it be granted to me who was a prisoner of the overwhelming desire for survival?

At the time, however, I was soon distracted. A Russian truck stopped and the soldiers offered us a lift. We accepted gratefully. They warned us to be careful around a *masło* barrel in the rear of the truck. *Masło* means butter in Polish, so we saw no reason for caution and thought the warning was a joke or a way to keep us from eating their butter. However, when the truck jolted over rough ground, we made an unpleasant linguistic discovery—*masło* means oil in Russian. I was wearing the only dress I owned and it was ruined. But we laughed and the soldiers laughed. It seemed nothing could spoil our elation.

But something did dampen our spirits. Shortly after we got off the Russian truck, another stopped for us, this one carrying Polish soldiers who wore a Polish eagle on their traditional four-cornered caps. It was a different eagle from the prewar emblem of the Polish state: it had no crown. Who cared? The young men, in the gallant Polish manner, got out to help us aboard. We were delighted to see our first Polish soldiers. We learned that they had been mobilized as part of the Second Polish Army, formed after the Russian Army and the Kosciuszko Division (now called the First Polish Army) had crossed the former Polish–Russian border. They were happy in the Army. The food was good, they said. They looked forward to following the Russian Army and fighting the Germans when their training period was over.

We told them that we were thinking about joining the Army. When they learned that Celinka was a physician and I was a lawyer, they became enthusiastic about our plans. "You have to do it! There are too many Jewish doctors in the Army hospitals."

"And you," they addressed me, "with your education, can easily get a lot of good positions. There are so many Jewish political officers. We hate those bastards."

"You will get nice uniforms," they added, trying not to stare at my dress, so recently smeared with *masło*.

My ruined dress did not bother me at all. But I was upset. Neither Celinka nor I set them straight. Not only did we not admit that we were Jewish, but we did not object to the reference to Jewish "bastards." Yet we were shocked. It was our rotten first encounter with the future Poland. But our minds, perhaps too flexible, found explanations: the soldiers had not been in the Army long enough to be reeducated, to be taught international brotherhood; they were still poisoned by the anti-Semitism of prewar Poland and the Nazi propaganda. The shock abated. However, this episode reinforced my tendency to keep my

secret and to be very cautious. This encounter should have
sent strong signals to me—at least that I should think seriously about what had happened. But I refused to hear
the first signals of anti-Semitism, and I would again decline
to accept them in the years to come. My Jewishness was
a threat to the happiness I longed for. So I brushed aside
everything that could spoil it, and I kept walking toward
Lublin with a strong hope that the future was going to
bring the new world of my dreams.

Lublin and Beyond

THE NEXT DAY, in the early afternoon, we reached Lublin, which had been proclaimed the temporary capital of the Polish People's Republic on July 22, 1944, by the Committee of National Liberation. The city was not damaged—the Germans had left before the Russians entered—but even in retreat the Nazis had taken the time to kill all the surviving prisoners in Majdanek, the notorious Lublin death camp. The city was very busy as refugees poured in from the west. Now that circumstances had changed, people had to find new means of livelihood, and much selling and bartering went on. The Russians were eager to pay for watches, lingerie, and other items considered great luxuries in the U.S.S.R.

Our first concern, Celinka's and mine, was to find a place to sleep. We knew no one in Lublin. In the hope of receiving an invitation from some resident, we went to a café and talked about our predicament loudly enough, as we sipped our tea, to be overheard by people sitting nearby. The trick worked. A matronly woman approached us, apologized for eavesdropping, and invited us to come home with her. We were exhausted and could hardly wait to take a shower. When we arrived and were shown into our room, I unbuttoned my dress and Celinka took a professional look at my chest—I had complained of pain and itching. She was very upset and said that I had scabies, which was highly contagious. We would have to go to a medical station first thing in the morning, since we couldn't expose our kind hostess to this unpleasant condition. However, when I took off my clothes, I found a big, fat louse—disgusting enough, but better than scabies. I laughed at Celinka's diagnosis. She was not too pleased; doctors usually don't like to admit errors, although this error was clearly to the patient's advantage.

The next day we walked the Lublin streets, hoping to encounter relatives or friends among the Polish soldiers or refugees. I was looking for my brother, who had worked just before the war as a junior partner in a law firm in Kolbuszowa, a small town close to the former eastern border of Poland and part of the territory the Russians had occupied in 1939. I had good reason to believe that he would be among the refugees or soldiers. It turned out he was still in Russia and would return to Poland a year later.

I noticed a colonel—in Polish uniform, obviously Jewish. I excused myself and asked if, by chance, he had met an

Ilja Rubinstein. The man seemed astonished, then burst out laughing: he turned out to be an old friend of mine—even a former admirer—whose name was also Rubinstein, though we were not related. I did not recognize him because he looked different in uniform, and we had not seen each other for many years. At the age of eighteen he had left Poland to join the International Brigade fighting against General Franco in Spain. He had escaped from a concentration camp, had gone to Russia, and had joined the Polish Army formed there, which was now stationed in Lublin.

Leon Rubinstein took Celinka and me to his house. Besides an unforgettable dinner, Leon's wife gave us clothes we badly needed. Another old friend, Roma Torunczyk, who lived with them, presented us with sturdy military boots—just in time, since our sabots were falling apart.

We had many surprising and touching encounters with friends who had returned from Russia. Some held high office in the new administration, and we were offered many good positions. But we stuck to our decision to join the Army. Soon Celinka was a doctor in a military hospital and I was an editor for *The White Eagle* (*Orzel Biały*), the newspaper of the Second Polish Army.

My experiences in the Army were rich and absorbing, but they are not part of this story. I will recall only one extraordinary moment. After Berlin fell, I drove there with my friends, Colonel Stefan Halicki and his wife, Genia, both Jewish. We left the car and walked to the Brandenburg Gate. Here was the Arch of Triumph through which haughty victorious German soldiers had goose-stepped to celebrate their glories and the humiliation of other nations.

I looked at the war-ravaged Arch. I was silent. So were my friends. It was one of the greatest moments in my life. Here was I, Zofia Rubinstein, a Jew sentenced to perish in the gas chambers, an Untermensch doomed to death. And here I was, standing in the heart of Berlin, in the uniform of a Polish officer.

In May 1945, I returned from Germany to Poland. Back in Lodz, I found the building where my family had lived. It was intact. The same janitor was there; he recognized me at once. He seemed embarrassed, or perhaps he was only surprised to see one of the Jewish tenants still alive. I went to our apartment, where two refugee families were living. I saw a few pieces of our family furniture—a chest of drawers and a wardrobe in my parents' bedroom, a cupboard in the living room.

In one room lived a Folksdeutsch who had occupied the whole apartment after my parents had been compelled to move into the ghetto. He seemed afraid of me. He tried to explain that he had not harmed my parents: they had to leave and their apartment was then allotted to him, an ethnic German. It was not his fault that he was of German extraction like so many other inhabitants of Lodz. He would not have objected if my parents had taken all their furniture. They just could not do it; the place in the ghetto was much too small. Did I want to take the rest of the furniture now?

I could not speak. I did not blame the man for moving into my parents' apartment. I was far from blaming him for accepting Folksdeutsch status. In Lodz, which had been incorporated into the Reich, people were not given choices. What was outrageous and repulsive was the fact

that he "offered" me my parents' furniture. How dare he?
I did not take anything. I couldn't. I had hoped to find
some pictures of my family, but there were none. If my
parents had left any, this man, the new occupant of the
apartment, would have thrown them into the trash. I left
my childhood home and never went back.

Since the Russians had taken Lodz without a single shot,
the buildings, streets, squares, and parks were all as they
had been before the war. Lodz was my birthplace, but for
me it had become a different city. The faces in the street
were unfamiliar; the Jewish stores, so characteristic of the
prewar midtown, had vanished. I remembered shopping
with my mother for shoes at Windman's, for dress materials
at Babiacki's.

In spite of the hopes I had nourished, I found not a
single member of my family. I was a total stranger in my
native town, and I felt very lonely. I did meet a few people
I had known before the war, among them a young captain
in the uniform of the Polish Army. He was slim, dark-
haired, with a smile in his gray eyes. I had seen him only
two or three times in my student days, but our paths had
crossed twice when we were soldiers—he in the First
Army, formed in Russia, I in the Second, formed in Lublin.
Now, all of a sudden, we encountered each other in Lodz.
I told him how glad I was to see him again, admitting that
I had thought of him over the years, more than would be
expected from our casual acquaintance. Half seriously, half
jokingly—it was his style—he told me that our encounters
had been unmistakable signs that we were a *zywyk*, a couple
determined by destiny. And he was probably right, because
very soon afterward we got married.

My husband later became the director of the national-
ized printing industry. He had been told by the Central
Committee of the party to change his Jewish name because
he held a high position in the administration. He was Kuba
Rapoport; thereafter he became Victor Kubar, his new
surname a compound of his first name and the first initial
of his true surname. I liked the new name; it was rather
neutral, not ostentatiously Polish, but by no means Jewish.
Consequently, I became Zofia Sielczak-Kubar by adding
my fictitious Polish name to my husband's. Instead of wel-
coming the chance to return to my family name, I abandoned Zofia Rubinstein forever, of my own free will. It
just sounded strange to my "refined" ear, jarring in the
Polish language I loved so much.

My marriage lasted twenty-four years, until I left Poland.
Those years were sometimes happy, now and then difficult,
never boring. We shared the joys of parenthood, the naïve
enthusiasm of the first years after the war, and the bitter
experiences of disappointment and disillusionment.

* * *

*My departure from Lodz and the move to Warsaw in 1946
closes the account of my wartime experiences. My own future—
my marriage and family; my work as a journalist, editor, and
author—is another story. Here I will say only that I left Poland
in March 1969, in the middle of the outrageous anti-Semitic
campaign organized by the Communist government. I finally
found the courage I had not found years earlier to make this
painful decision. My two daughters left several months ahead
of me; my husband refused to leave. My family life was ruined.
My dream world had fallen apart. I applied for permission to*

emigrate, received my travel document,* and left. I left my country. I left my past.

But the fate of the friends I depended on for my survival, whose joys and sorrows I perceived as my own, is part of this story and it is time to call the roll.

*   *   *

* Jews who emigrated had to renounce their citizenship. They did not receive passports, only a travel document stating that the bearer was not a Polish citizen. This document expired two days after the bearer crossed the Polish border.

Farewell to Danka

AFTER THE LIBERATION, people were returning to Warsaw and leaving written messages for their relatives and friends in the rubble of their former houses. That was how, in a roundabout way, I learned about Danka's whereabouts. She was no longer in Zanęcin, the village where I had left her eight months before. The neighbor's baby had died soon after we set out for Lublin; since the man no longer needed Danka to nurse his child, he abandoned her. The peasants also made it clear that she had enjoyed their hospitality long enough. Carrying Tolek, she wandered the countryside in search of work and shelter.

Now she was staying at the estate of a gentry family. They exploited her mercilessly, giving her nothing but a room and a little food in exchange for hard work. I had to get her out of there as soon as possible. It was very difficult. I had no place of my own. Mrs. Uklejska came to the rescue once more; she asked one of her former teachers, who managed an orphanage in Stettin, to help Danka. People never turned down Mrs. Uklejska's requests. The woman hired Danka, and she and Tolek were assured of a decent place to live.

A few months later, I received a letter from Danka asking me to make other arrangements for her. The climate in Stettin, a Baltic port, was bad for Tolek, who had contracted tuberculosis during their ordeal in the last months of the war. She also felt lonely and wanted to be closer to me.

It was very difficult to find a place for Danka. Warsaw was rebuilding rapidly, but apartments had been allotted to people with important government jobs or to those considered indispensable in restoring the city to life. Although Lodz had not been destroyed, it was vastly overcrowded; most of the government agencies had been located there temporarily until they could be moved to the capital. I was living with my husband in a prewar hotel in Lodz, waiting for an apartment to be rehabilitated in a bombed-out building in Warsaw.

It seemed to me that the place for Danka was a hospital, where she could work and find lodging in the same building. She could be trained on the job to become a practical nurse and would then be able to earn a decent living. I found such a hospital nearby, under the administration of the Internal Security Service; more precisely, I found a doctor working there who had been a close friend of my family's. Dr. Leon Altman agreed to present Danka's case to the personnel department of the hospital. He and I endorsed her application, emphasizing her courage and magnanimity in helping the Jews.

I also vouched for her as deserving a special clearance, since this hospital treated employees of the Internal Security Service. Danka was soon given a job with the prospect of practical training, a room in the hospital building, and a place for Tolek in the infants' day nursery. No better arrangement could have been made.

A few days later, she arrived in Lodz. I managed to smuggle her into our hotel room for the night. In the morning, she left for the routine physical examination and other formalities required of new employees.

A week passed. One afternoon the door of our hotel room burst open and Danka ran in. She threw herself on a chair, crying bitterly. Between sobs she told me that the test for venereal disease had been positive: the diagnosis was syphilis. She was told that a job in the hospital was out of the question.

She swore no man had touched her since Tolek's birth, and that the test for venereal diseases routinely performed before the delivery had been negative. How could she have contracted the disease? Dr. Altman sent Danka once again to a specialist. During the interview with the doctor, Danka recalled that once she'd had a kind of chancre, or "ulcer," on her breast and that it had developed after the neighbor's child had bitten her while she was nursing him. That was it—a syphilitic chancre. The child had had syphilis and infected Danka, a rare case of syphilis not transmitted by sexual intercourse. The doctor inquired further about the chancre and about the infant's appearance. When she described him as extremely ugly—grotesque—the doctor had no doubt. How could Danka have known about such a danger? I had endorsed the idea of nursing a motherless child as a natural and human deed. There was a great irony of fate in Danka's miseries. She was so often mistreated by the very people she helped, or, as in this case, was hurt because she had been good to someone.

The puzzle of Danka's syphilis had been solved, but not the problem of what to do. Once more I went to Dr. Altman and begged him to intervene with the personnel department; the circumstances were so unusual and Danka was a person who deserved to be helped. At first, Dr. Altman did not want to listen. The hospital had made the right decision. The situation was also extremely awkward for him. To understand his position, one must appreciate the paranoia in the internal security agencies. They could even have accused him of deliberately misleading the hospital authorities; this could be considered a political crime.

However, Dr. Altman was kindhearted and courageous. He understood that there was no other way for Danka. She had to work, she had to have a place to live, and she had to have treatment. He finally convinced the personnel department to give Danka a job in the hospital storeroom, where all contact with patients could be avoided. Ultimately Danka was entirely cured.

Danka's stay in the hospital lasted less than two years. She was fired—paradoxically—because of anti-Semitism. It happened this way. Employees of the secret police agencies received yard goods, clothes, and other supplies in addition to their salary. Most of these goods were acquired during searches of suspects. Some were appropriated by the officials making the search and some were distributed. Once Danka argued that several yards of material should have been given to her and not to another woman, who happened to be Jewish. Jewish employees were better treated than Gentiles, Danka said angrily. And she was denounced for this remark and fired. Reporting on colleagues was encouraged by the authorities: it was even considered a proof of loyalty and devotion to socialist principles.

It was easy to understand that Danka's remark did not make her an anti-Semite. It was the way many Poles used to talk: "You sound like a Jew, you have nerves like a Jew, greedy as a Jew," and so on. So did Danka sometimes; it was the way she was brought up. However, in 1947 the myth of international brotherhood was strongly maintained by the government and the party. Danka had to be punished. I received a summons from the secret police headquarters on Koszykowa Street to testify in her case. I told them how generously and courageously she had helped the Jews during the German occupation. They did not accept my testimony. Danka was fired and after some time found a job in a textile factory.

We had learned that our apartment in Warsaw was ready and my husband and I left Lodz. Danka visited us in Warsaw and I went back to see her in Lodz. She never failed to bring flowers and a small gift for me or my children.

A year later, Danka married. I learned that she was pregnant and that the father was a gardener employed in the hospital garden. Danka had become interested in Bernard because he was Jewish; she was convinced, as I have noted, that Jews were superior to Gentiles. In her short life, one disappointment had followed another, sometimes because of her circumstances, sometimes because of her naïveté. Unfortunately, she had rarely met honest and good people before she met my Jewish friends. So she concluded that Bernard, since he was Jewish, was a suitable partner for her. And he was a kindhearted man, who would turn out to be tender and considerate to Danka, and a devoted father to Tolek and to their daughter, Barbara.

As long as I remained in Poland, I was in steady contact with Danka and Bernard. Although they lived in poverty, she would never accept money from me. Once when she was hospitalized she asked me to send 500 zlotys to Bernard. I sent the money and wrote her that she need not hurry to repay it because I had recently published a book and was well off. But as soon as she received the delayed disability payment, she repaid the debt. Fortunately, she let herself be convinced that presents could be accepted. I would send clothing and other necessities her family could not afford. Danka used to say that I owed her no gratitude for what she had done for me. It was I, she said, who was always so good. So we both kept sending presents. Sometimes her uncritical admiration irritated me. It made me feel uneasy, even slightly guilty.

When I left Poland, Danka wept. She was sick and aging and had little to look forward to. Her husband was to die a few years later. She once said to me, "You would never disappoint me. I love you. If you had disappointed me, I would have stopped believing that honesty and justice existed." I was the one she believed could help her in her predicaments, the only one who would never let her down. Had I let her down? I sometimes ask myself the question.

I wrote her about my battle with cancer. What a wonderful letter she sent back! She reminded me that I had once told her that after the war my parents would have two daughters, Danka and me.

"Your parents did not survive," she wrote, "but it was so beautiful to have dreamed that I would have parents. I never knew my mother. But you are my sister. Please write often and tell me how you are feeling. Your sister in Lodz is waiting impatiently for news from you."

Presences and Absences

FROM THE SMALL GROUP which escaped from the column driven to the cattle cars on January 18, 1943, when the story began, only Tosia and Marcel Reich-Ranicki and I survived. I have already reported that Gustava Jarecka, the brilliant writer and our dear friend who refused to escape with us, died from suffocation in the train. Recently I found a description of her last hours in the memoirs of Stanisław Adler (*In the Warsaw Ghetto, 1940–1943: An Account of a Witness*):

Alter [a friend of the author] held on to the window desperately, standing on a pile of corpses. His brother Mieczysław was losing his remaining strength. To place him at the window for a breath of fresh air, Alter had to enlarge the macabre pyramid [of corpses]. For this purpose, he began pulling a corpse by the leg. When he heard a moan, he bent over and recognized the novelist Jarecka. Moments later, she breathed her last breath. Alter chose a moment to jump out of the window of the freight car. He returned to Warsaw two days later.

Tosia and Marcel Reich-Ranicki survived the Nazi occupation on the Aryan side. I really owe Marcel my life. If it hadn't been for his determination and presence of mind, I would never have escaped the deportation. The Reich-Ranickis left Poland in 1956; a brilliant critic and an authority on German literature, Marcel is now chief editor of the book section of the *Frankfurter Allgemeine Zeitung*. We correspond from time to time; he once sent me a picture of Gustava Jarecka which he had managed to keep through the occupation.

Stefa, the friend who found my first refuge with Miss Okonska, contracted tuberculosis during the war. Afterward, her husband, Szczęsny Dobrowolski, took her to Switzerland, where she died. I met her brother, Daniel Prywes, in Israel in 1970. He asked my opinion about exhuming her remains and burying her in the cemetery of the kibbutz Maale Hamisha: how would Stefa have regarded this move, since she had been a Communist? I told him I felt strongly that she would have approved of being buried in Israel. Stefa had been misled by the Communists and would surely have changed her mind. She was a brave fighter in the underground and deserved to find her eternal peace in the kibbutz. So she was buried in the Maale Hamisha cemetery.

Stefa's husband, Szczęsny Dobrowolski, who had smuggled himself into the ghetto to persuade me and others to escape to the Aryan side, was one of those Poles who devoted themselves to an uncompromising struggle against anti-Semitism. I have quoted his newspaper criticism of the attitude of the Poles toward the Jews during the ghetto uprising. His courage in the underground was widely known. However, history was not kind to this generous and brave man. Immediately after the war, he held a high position as deputy to the editor in chief of *The People's Tribune (Trybuna Ludu)*, the newspaper of the Central Committee of the Polish Workers' Party. In 1951, following the arrest on false charges of Władysław Gomułka, the party's Secretary General, Szczęsny was arrested and spent several years in a Communist prison. He was freed and "rehabilitated" after Stalin's death, but died soon afterward from cancer.

Cesia Szczypińska, my schoolmate who was so helpful to me and to other Jews, still lives in Warsaw. She married her fiancé, Jerzy Jelinski, who returned after the war from London. Our friendship survived in spite of our past differences of political opinion. She had been right. Her daughters, each a year junior to my two, were named after them—a token of our friendship. She told me that Max, the head of the currency ring in the flea market at Kercelak, had died a hero's death in the Warsaw uprising. It was Max who had tried to help rescue Stefan, Helena Brodowska's boyfriend.

My dear friend Helena Brodowska, the other tenant in Mrs. Kałużniacka's house, who studied history so ardently, was, until her recent retirement, a professor of history at the University of Lodz. She has sent me a number of the books she has published on the history of the Polish peasantry. She did not have an easy career, because she did not join the party. I have told how she helped me and her fellow students and professors during the occupation, and how, more than twenty years later, during the anti-Semitic campaign in 1967–70, she again defended her Jewish fellow teachers who were ousted from their jobs.

Until I left Poland, I remained in close contact with my landladies on Dobrogniewa Street. After I left, Helena sent news of them. Recently she wrote me that Mrs. Kałuż-niacka, in her nineties and blind, had died in a home for the aged run by nuns. Her sister, Janina, had also passed away.

My friend Marysia refused to leave Warsaw before the uprising, because of the responsibility she felt for her pa-tient, the old countess. She shared the fate of many other Warsavians, sent to work in German factories and confined in concentration camps. Marysia was in Ravensbrück until May 1945, when the prisoners were liberated by American troops.

After the war, she emigrated to the United States. We met again in 1971, when I came to America as an immi-grant, and we still visit each other. She is warm and helpful, as always. We speak about the old days; often we talk of Celinka, who was a devoted and compassionate doctor until her death in Sweden some years ago.

I met Zula Sterling, my housemate in the villa in Radość, in an odd way shortly after the war. She came to the hotel in Lodz where my husband and I were staying. She was to be interviewed by Victor for a position as his secretary. When I opened the door of our hotel room, she was flabbergasted. "Zula, be careful," I said with mock severity. "You see before you the wife of your prospective boss."

We laughed and embraced. Needless to say, she got the job.

When we moved to Warsaw, Zula and her mother Anya were given an apartment next door to ours. Anya became the beloved "Granny" to my daughters; Zula, their dear "Auntie"—both of them my lifelong friends. Anya died in her eighties in Poland. Zula and her husband, Józek, emigrated to Sweden. Their son lives nearby; their daughter is in California.

Mrs. Uklejska remained my best friend, teacher, adviser, and confessor. She was the most remarkable person I have ever met. She was a mathematician and a psychologist, with wide knowledge of the humanities as well. I admired her brilliant mind. In her late seventies she wrote a remarkable book on the history of science. Yet she never tried to impress anyone. She was always natural and modest; she taught me the real meaning of tolerance. A person of the highest moral standards, she yet understood the need to compromise under certain conditions. There was nothing dogmatic about her. She understood human nature.

Once I came to her, dissatisfied with myself. I don't remember exactly what the problem was. As always, she listened carefully. This time she did not answer immediately, but found her own way to relate to the question. She reached for a book on the shelves, Thomas Mann's *Joseph and His Brothers*. Very quickly she found the paragraph she wanted. I remember it very well:

Hell is for the pure; that is the law of the moral world. For it is for sinners, and one can sin only against one's purity. If one is like the beasts of the field, one cannot sin, one knows no hell. Thus it is arranged, and hell is quite certainly

inhabited by the better sort; which is not just—but then
what is our justice?

We both laughed. She had a short, warm way of laughing
and she laughed often. I always admired her subtle and
wise sense of humor. Now, not only was I granted "ab-
solution" by the Egyptian philosopher through his speech
to Joseph, but I enjoyed the intellectual stimulation of Mrs.
Uklejska's company. She was a wonderful conversation-
alist. She knew many stories from the period·between the
wars, since she had been related to or acquainted with
several prominent political and literary figures. I learned
a lot about the unofficial history of Poland through her
stories. Amazingly, she never repeated herself.

On special occasions at her house, I met her Jewish
students among the guests. She continued to help them,
although the circumstances now were different. She never
mentioned her assistance. When I came to tell her that I
intended to emigrate, she approved of my decision.

"I will miss you," she said.

I miss her all the time.

Her daughters wrote to me when she died in 1979.
There was something extraordinary about her death, as
there was about her life. She was at church with her daughters, at a Mass commemorating the anniversary of her
brother's death. He had been a professor of theology at
the university in Lvov. She seemed quite well. Suddenly,
very quietly, she said that she felt ill. In a moment everything was over. By the time the doctor arrived, she had
died peacefully in her children's arms.

I have no mystical bent, but I felt as if angels had been
sent to the church to take her beautiful soul and save her

from suffering. Two of her former students wrote that they also felt something unearthly in her departure from this earthly life.

My parents stayed in the Lodz ghetto until the last deportation, which began August 3, 1944, and lasted until the end of the month. They died in the gas chambers of Auschwitz or Treblinka. This I learned after the war from my schoolmate Helena Lifszyc, who survived Auschwitz. She saw them frequently in the ghetto. The hope that my brother and I would survive, she told me, had helped my parents to endure their immense suffering.

I saw them for the last time in November 1939.

One of my last visits before I left Warsaw was to the Jewish cemetery. I had been asked to care for the grave of my cousin Bolesław Szenfeld by his mother, Rachela, who had emigrated to Australia in 1950. Bolesław had died a hero's death defending a barricade during the Warsaw uprising; he had been buried in the courtyard of a nearby building. After the war his mother had exhumed his remains and buried him in the Jewish cemetery. Now I had to go there to say goodbye to him and arrange with the Jewish congregation official for the care of the grave after my departure.

This was the saddest cemetery ever seen. In the foreground are a few graves which are more or less tidied up, apparently to prove that the custodian earns his salary. The heroes of the Warsaw ghetto uprising are buried here. Not far away is the grave, also fairly well tended, of Adam Czerniakow, the chairman of the Judenrat, who had committed suicide to protest the deportation in 1942.

Beyond are many unmarked graves: these are of the people buried by Pinkiert's, the undertakers who flourished during the war. Those found dead of starvation on the streets of the ghetto, or shot by the Germans, lie there. It is difficult to get to the rest of the cemetery: one must go through a jungle of high grass and weeds covering the fallen and broken monuments. In the oldest part of the cemetery are buried the people who died before the war. Here one can read names, dates, and inscriptions of love.

Of all those buried in this graveyard, I knew only my cousin. Most of those I loved—my parents, uncles, aunts, cousins, and friends—have no burial place except in my heart, where I tend a private cemetery.

Acknowledgments

"Mother, you promised to write your story," my daughters kept saying. Thank you, Joanna and Małgosia, for your persistence and your faith in me.

I would like to express my deep appreciation and gratitude to Dr. Kristen Ries, who took care of me so devotedly during my illness. She urged me to start writing as soon as I was taken off the critical list.

My appreciation to Zina Davis, the typist and first reader of the manuscript. During my recovery, she would come by to pick up the handwritten pages and was so eager to read the subsequent part of the story that I had to have the next portion ready for her.

My very special thanks to Ruth Mathewson for her precious friendship. She greatly improved the quality of my English—the language of the country I have chosen as my own. She was generous with her time, suggestions, and attention. Thanks to her and Jean Hanff Korelitz, my manuscript landed on the desk of Steve Wasserman, my invaluable publisher. My gratitude to him, to my editor Paul Golob, and to all the friendly staff of Hill and Wang.